Mindsets
in the
Classroom

The latest edition of *Mindsets in the Classroom* provides educators with ideas and strategies to build a growth mindset school culture, wherein students are challenged to change their thinking about their abilities and potential through resilience, perseverance, and a variety of strategies.

This updated edition contains content from the first and second edition, eliminates content that is no longer relevant, and adds a layer of learning that has occurred since the original publication: lessons learned through more recent brain research, implementation of the concept by educators across the world, as well as the author's own observations and reflections after working in schools, coaching educators, and talking with teachers, administrators, parents, and students about their own mindsets.

With this book's easy-to-follow advice, tasks, and strategies, teachers can grow a love of learning while facilitating the development of resilient, successful students.

Mary Cay Ricci is an education consultant and speaker. She was previously an elementary and middle school teacher and central office administrator in three large school districts. She holds certification in gifted and talented education and administration and supervision from Johns Hopkins University, where she was previously a faculty associate in the Graduate School of Education.

Mindsets
in the
Classroom

Building a Culture of Success and Student Achievement in Schools

Third Edition

Mary Cay Ricci

Routledge
Taylor & Francis Group

NEW YORK AND LONDON

PRUFROCK PRESS INC.

WACO, TEXAS

Third edition published 2024
by Routledge
605 Third Avenue, New York, NY 10158

and by Routledge
4 Park Square, Milton Park, Abingdon, Oxon, OX14 4RN

Routledge is an imprint of the Taylor & Francis Group, an informa business

First published in 2013 by Prufrock Press Inc.
Second edition published in 2021 by Routledge

Library of Congress Cataloging-in-Publication Data
Names: Ricci, Mary Cay, 1960- author.
Title: Mindsets in the classroom: building a growth mindset learning community/Mary Cay Ricci.
Description: Third edition. | New York, NY: Routledge, 2024. | Includes bibliographical references.
Identifiers: LCCN 2023054831 (print) | LCCN 2023054832 (ebook) | ISBN 9781032525006 (hardback) | ISBN 9781032524955 (paperback) | ISBN 9781003406914 (ebook)
Subjects: LCSH: Learning, Psychology of. | Academic achievement. | Motivation in education.
Classification: LCC LB1060 .R495 2024 (print) | LCC LB1060 (ebook) | DDC 370.15/23—dc23/eng/20231211
LC record available at https://lccn.loc.gov/2023054831
LC ebook record available at https://lccn.loc.gov/2023054832

ISBN: 978-1-032-52500-6 (hbk)
ISBN: 978-1-032-52495-5 (pbk)
ISBN: 978-1-003-40691-4 (ebk)

DOI: 10.4324/9781003406914

Typeset in Garamond
By Deanta Global Publishing Services, Chennai, India

For my children—Christopher, Patrick, and Isabella. You continue to inspire me. May you always believe that with effort and perseverance you can do anything.

For my late parents—Joe and Mary Ellen Marchione. Thank you for believing in me.

For Enio—Thank you for your support and patience.

For the people in my professional life who saw things in me that I did not see in myself—Ginny, Carl, and Monique.

Contents

About the Author

Mary Cay Ricci is an education author, consultant, and keynote speaker. She is the author of the *New York Times* best-selling education book, *Mindsets in the Classroom: Building a Growth Mindset Learning Community* and its partner books, the 2016 Legacy Book Award winner, *Ready-to-Use Resources for Mindsets in the Classroom*, coauthor of *Mindsets for Parents: Strategies to Encourage Growth Mindset in Kids*, children's book, *Nothing You Can't Do! The Secret Power of Growth Mindsets*, and to round off the series, *Create a Growth Mindset School: An Administrators Guide to Leading a Growth Mindset Community*.

Mary Cay is a popular keynote speaker and enjoys working with school districts across the country. She was previously an elementary and middle school teacher, the Supervisor for Advanced and Enriched Instruction for Prince George's County Public Schools, MD; Coordinator of Advanced Academics for Baltimore County Public Schools; and an instructional specialist in the Division of Enriched and Accelerated Instruction for Montgomery County Public Schools, MD. Mary Cay holds a master's degree that includes certification in Gifted and Talented Education and Administration and Supervision from Johns Hopkins University, where she was previously a faculty associate in the Graduate School of Education. She completed her undergraduate degree in elementary education at Mercyhurst University. Mary Cay previously served on the CEC-TAG board of directors for eight years. Her greatest achievement, however, is her three children, Christopher, Patrick, and Isabella, from whom she has learned the most.

CHAPTER 1

WHAT ARE MINDSETS, AND HOW DO THEY AFFECT THE CLASSROOM?

"Look at her paper—she's the smart one!" It was the first month of school in a third-grade classroom, and I was visiting the students to see if they had any prior knowledge about the brain. This particular school had a 70% poverty/FARMS rate (Free and Reduced Meals), and the majority of students did not have English as their first language. As I circulated around the tables, I was observing a student writing copiously when I heard it: "Look at her paper—she's the smart one!" This announcement proudly came from one of her classmates. When I assured him that he along with his classmates were all working hard on the assignment, he agreed, but again shared that this particular classmate would have the best paper.

DOI: 10.4324/9781003406914-1

What I discovered in this classroom was a profound example of a fixed mindset at play—an eight-year-old child who believed that his classmate was the "smart one," and that no matter the amount of hard work he put in, her work would always be better. That's where this book comes in—to help the many teachers, administrators, coaches, parents, and students like the one in this scenario realize that they can change the way they think about success and intelligence in the classroom.

Since the original *Mindsets in the Classroom* book was published in 2013 and updated in 2018, we have learned more about the impact of mindsets on teaching and learning. This updated edition contains content from the first and second edition, eliminates content that is no longer relevant, and adds a layer of learning that has occurred since that time: lessons learned through more recent brain research, implementation of the concept by educators across the world, as well as my own observations and reflections after working in schools, coaching educators, and talking with teachers, administrators, parents, and students about their own mindsets. We will continually learn more about the impact of mindsets as we implement practices into educational settings. If you are already familiar with the concept of fixed and growth mindset, go ahead and skim or skip the first part of this chapter, as it provides an explanation of growth and fixed mindsets.

Can Intelligence Be Changed?

What Are Growth Mindsets and Fixed Mindsets? The belief that intelligence, talents, and skills are malleable and can be developed is not a new concept. However, the idea that intelligence can grow in both children and adults has seen more popularity in recent years thanks to the work of Stanford University professor of psychology, Dr. Carol Dweck, and her 2006 book, *Mindset: The New Psychology of Success*. Dweck's research and development of the fixed and growth mindset theory has contributed to a major shift in thinking about many aspects of life. I have taken her research and applied it more specifically to teaching and learning.

Dweck (2006) described a belief system that asserts that intelligence and talent are malleable and can be developed—she coined the term *growth mindset* to describe this belief system. Learners who employ growth mindset thinking believe that with perseverance, resiliency, and a variety of strategies, they can learn and improve. There might be some struggle and failure along the way, but they understand that with deliberate effort and perseverance, they can succeed. The focus of a growth mindset individual is on the process of learning and growing, not on looking smart or even the final outcome or grade. An educator with a growth mindset believes that with effort, hard work, and application of strategies from the learner, all students can demonstrate significant growth and therefore all students deserve challenging instructional opportunities. Add to this belief an effective teacher armed with instructional tools that differentiate, respond to learners' needs, and nurture critical thinking processes, and you have a recipe for optimum student learning.

Growth mindset

a belief system that suggests that one's intelligence and/or talents can be grown or developed with persistence, effort, and a focus on learning

Dweck also presents a different belief system about intelligence: the belief that intelligence, skills, and talents are something you are born with and the level of intelligence cannot be changed—*a fixed mindset*. A person who exhibits fixed mindset thinking might truly believe that they have a predetermined amount of intelligence, skills, or talents. This belief system is problematic at both ends of the continuum. For those students who struggle or do not perceive themselves as "smart," it becomes a self-fulfilling prophecy. Because they don't really believe that they can be successful, they will often give up and not put forth effort. For those students who are advanced learners, they can become consumed with "looking smart" at all costs. They may have coasted through school without really putting forth much effort, yet they are often praised for their good grades and strong skills. Often, an advanced learner with a fixed mindset will start avoiding situations where they may fail; they can become "risk-averse."

Think for a minute about your own mindset. A mindset is a set of personal beliefs and is a way of thinking that influences your behavior and attitude toward yourself and others. An educator's mindset directly influences how a child feels about themself and how they view themselves as a learner. A child's mindset directly affects how he or she faces academic challenges. A child who utilizes growth mindset thinking perseveres even in the face of difficulty. A child who engages in fixed mindset thinking may give up easily, lack resiliency, and not engage in the learning process.

A fixed or growth mindset can directly affect family dynamics as well. It is not surprising to note that parents also have a big impact on how children view themselves. They will often view their children through specific lenses: "Joseph was born knowing his math facts," "Domenic has always asked good questions," and "Catherine has always known how to interpret a piece of literature." These are all examples of a fixed mindset, even though the statements sound positive. These statements describe who these children "are," not the effort that they have put forth. As educators, think of some occasions when you have heard a parent describe her child in a way that rationalizes perceived weaknesses: "She is just like me; math was not my thing either" or "I can understand why he does not do well in reading; I never liked to read." (Ideas and resources for helping parents embrace a growth mindset will be discussed in

Chapter 6, or readers can pick up *Mindsets for Parents: Strategies to Encourage Growth Mindsets in Kids* Ricci & Lee, 2024.)

Shifting Mindsets

Breaking down the belief that intelligence is pre-determined at birth can be a challenge, but with the proper groundwork, education, and some time to observe and reflect, a mindset can shift little by little. Expecting a shift in mindset immediately is not realistic; after all, some of us have had fixed mindset beliefs for most of our lives. Even after someone has had a self-proclaimed mindset shift, they will need to make a conscious effort to maintain that belief. I have studied this work since 2008, given hundreds of talks and presentations, and at times still find myself fighting internal fixed mindset thinking. The truth of the matter is that we all have an area (or two or three) in our lives where we tend to have a fixed mindset—those times when we say to ourselves, "I could never… (fill in the blank)," or "I am terrible at…" Take cooking, for example. Have you ever heard someone state that they are a terrible cook? I would argue that just about anyone can learn to cook basic dishes if they put in the time, effort, and practice into learning how—the question is, do they have the motivation to want to put in the time, effort, and practice in order to learn how to cook?

Even in areas where you have a growth mindset, a fixed mindset can have an elasticity that continually wants to spring back. For example, a twice-exceptional child (a "gifted" student with learning challenges) called to share a college schedule with his mother who also happened to be an educator. The parent had a mindset "shift" several years ago and had proudly told me all she did to encourage a growth mindset culture within their home. The schedule her son shared involved 8 a.m. classes and a course roster that included macroeconomics, international business, accounting, analysis of media, and management. His mother noted that the fixed mindset mentality buried within her wanted to scream, "Are you crazy? You are setting yourself up for failure!" Instead, she responded, "It sounds like a challenging schedule, and I know that with continued effort, you will be able to manage it." Believing that all children can, with effort, perseverance, and a good set of strategies, succeed is the heart of this belief.

Brain-Based Research

One of the reasons for this shift in thinking about intelligence is due to the available technology that examines the function and makeup of the brain. Neuroscience has had a significant impact on teaching and learning. Brain research dismisses the notion that intelligence is "fixed" from birth. Both formal and informal studies demonstrate that the brain can develop with the proper stimulus. A big focus in neuroscience emphasizes the concept of neuroplasticity. Neuroplasticity is the ability of the brain to change, adapt, and "rewire" itself throughout our entire life. Anyone who has ever witnessed someone recovering from a brain injury or stroke has had a front-row seat to watching neuroplasticity. In the case of a stroke, for most patients, the brain begins the rewiring process almost immediately so that patients learn to speak and become mobile again. However, it often takes the hard work and effort put forth in occupational, physical, and speech therapy for stroke patients to make significant progress. Neuroplasticity works both ways; it creates new connections and weakens or eliminates connections that are not used very often. When neurons are eliminated, it is called synaptic pruning. Synaptic pruning is the process in which neurons that are not being used are eliminated to increase brain efficiency. This process mostly occurs between early childhood and puberty. However, newer research suggests that synaptic pruning can continue into a person's late twenties.

Neuroplasticity

the ability of the brain to change, adapt, and "rewire" itself throughout our entire lifelife

We now know so much more about the neurological aspects of the brain that it cannot help but inform the way we approach learning and instruction. This understanding directly affects teachers' beliefs and expectations about student potential and achievement. It is when educators and children (as well as their parents) learn about the brain and all of its potential and when they witness the impact that it has on learning that mindsets can begin to shift (see Chapter 8 for ideas about teaching children about the brain).

Intelligence and Measuring Intelligence

Is it possible to increase your IQ? The University of Michigan partnered with the University of Bern to conduct a study that looked at the possibility of increasing IQ. This study (see Palmer, 2011) required participants to continually play a computerized memory game that involved remembering visual patterns. Each time a different pattern appeared, the participants heard a letter from the alphabet in their headphones. They were asked to respond when either the visual pattern on the screen or the letters they were hearing in their headphones were repeated. The time between the repeating of patterns and letters became longer as the game became more difficult. The researchers found that as the participants had practice and got better at the game, scores on IQ-style tests increased (Palmer, 2011).

This research, as well as other studies, contributes to the understanding of malleable intelligence, a key factor in growth mindset and a concept many educators struggle with. In general, educators do not have a lot of background in cognitive science. I asked several groups of educators the following question: "What do cognitive abilities tests/IQ tests measure?" Without exception, there was hesitancy in responding to the question; after giving sufficient wait time, a few responses were shared: "a child's capability," "how smart they are," and "their innate ability." What surprised me more than the inaccurate responses was the observation that so many of these teachers and administrators just could not answer the question. There are many times educators are in situations where data is shared about a student, and that data often includes cognitive scores from gifted and talented screening processes, special education screening processes, and/or IQ tests. Who knew so many educators really have no idea what these assessments actually measure?

Cognitive ability tests measure *developed* ability. Therefore, if a child has never had an opportunity to develop the kinds of reasoning processes that these assessments measure, the outcome of one of these assessments would not be meaningful. When parents and educators review these "intelligence" scores, assumptions may be made about the child, and beliefs may kick in that place limits on the child's potential.

The Role of Potential and Hard Work

Potential. What a great word. It is all about possibilities. However, "potential" is often used in ways that can make me slightly uncomfortable. Think of the phrase, "He is not working to his full potential" or "We will help your child reach their full potential." How does potential become "full"? Is it something that can be checked off on a report card? Potential can never be "full"; it is never-ending and our possibilities are infinite. As a person grows, learning and experiences become more sophisticated and challenging, growth continually occurs, and potential is never reached because it is impossible to reach. Perhaps many thought Michael Phelps reached his "full" potential after earning his 16th Olympic medal in 2008—a feat he went on to shatter at the 2012 Olympics when he won six more medals, and then won an additional six in 2016. Believing that intelligence, talent, skills, and, yes, even athletic ability can be developed encourages these endless possibilities.

We are all born with potential. However, we might have some innate strength or capacity in one or more specific areas. These strengths can manifest themselves in many ways. Strengths can be shown physically, creatively, socially, academically—the possibilities are endless. Some children are born with a greater degree of specific strengths compared to their peer group. For those children with outstanding specific strengths, their strengths deserve to be further developed.

> *However, it is also important to con-sider that all children have the potential to work side-by-side or even surpass those with intrinsic abilities.*

Many educators don't realize that approximately 75% of achieve-ment is attributed to psychosocial skills (which some researchers refer to as noncognitive factors) and only approximately 25% of innate intelligence or IQ contributes to achievement (Olszewski-Kubilius, 2013). The cultivation of these skills is imperative, espe-cially for those students who have not yet developed their abilities and/or talents. The skills that must be deliberately modeled, taught, and cultivated include, but are not limited to, perseverance, resil-iency, optimism, comfort with intellectual tension/discourse, cop-ing skills when faced with failure, and the ability to handle critique and constructive feedback (Olszewski-Kubilius, 2013).

Think about a student who has strong innate abilities—they learn quickly and give accurate responses in class. What if this student lacked perseverance and resiliency? As soon as things get challenging or they are not finding success easily, they disengage. It would not matter how strong their innate abilities are if they have not developed perseverance and resiliency; their achievement would suffer. The opposite is also true—think of a student whose innate abilities (according to a test) are "average" (a word I really don't like using, but one that works for illustrative purposes), but they show strength in perseverance and resiliency. This student can work side-by-side with those students whose innate abilities are stronger because they have the motivation and has developed important noncognitive skills in order to stick with and embrace challenge.

Think of a time that it took you a little longer to learn a new skill. It may have been something that required physical coordina-tion, playing a musical instrument, using a new kind of technology, or learning a new instructional strategy. Then, once you learned this new skill, it became a strength for you. In fact, you surpassed many others who have had this skill for years. As an adult, you had the drive, motivation, and persistence to decide that reaching this goal was important to you. No one took away the opportunity to let you learn, no one told you it was "too hard" for you, and no one told you that this was "not the right group" for you. No one put up barriers to hinder your learning.

Yet, sometimes our education system does all of the above. Our school structures eliminate opportunities, communicate low expectations, and prematurely remove students from challenging environments. Many reasons exist for hampering student potential in this way; one major obstacle is how we judge both adults and children by the speed with which things are completed.

Our society has become one that values pace. The faster, the better. If we don't get our large, oat milk, extra hot, caramel latte in less than two minutes, then we are annoyed. If our Wi-Fi connection is not instant, then we grumble or click fast and furiously. If a driver in front of us is not going at a pace we agree with, then we use the horn or moan out loud. If an educator describes a bright child in his classroom or school, then we might hear him refer to the child as "quick" and those in the bottom reading group as "slow."

We need to step back, take a breath, and realize that it is not about how fast students master learning. It is about the perseverance and effort that they put forth and the strategies that they utilize.

Growing School Communities That Embrace a Growth Mindset

Developing ways to establish a classroom or school community that promotes the belief that intelligence is malleable is the major goal of this book. The entire school staff—administrators, teachers, paraeducators, support staff—as well as parents must truly believe that all children can be successful. At the same time, children must also accept this belief system.

It is all about beliefs and expectations. One way that contributes greatly to both children and adults embracing this belief system is learning about the brain and all of its possibilities (again, see Chapter 8 for learning tasks that both children and adults can use to learn more about the brain). Neuroscience has grown by leaps and bounds in the last several years, and educating ourselves and our students about the brain has a huge impact on student effort and motivation.

Why Mindset Matters in Schools

Carol Dweck (2006) conducted a study of middle school math students in New York City. The students showed positive growth when they believed that intelligence is malleable and when they learned about their brains. Studies have shown that many students enter middle school with the belief that we are all born with a specific, set-in-stone intelligence level or a fixed mindset (Dweck, 2006). Similarly, it was shared with me that in one Washington, DC, suburban school working on changing its students' mindsets, it was determined through student feedback and interviews that more than 60% of the children entering grade 6 believed that they were born with specific academic strengths and weaknesses and that they could not change. *Based on this statistic*, I asked myself, *at what point do children really begin to believe this about themselves?*

This prompted me to undertake my own studies. I began collecting data in kindergarten classes. In the fall, kindergarten students were surveyed to capture their beliefs about intelligence. The following statements, which have been adapted from *Mindset Works* (www.mindsetworks.com), were used with students in grades K–3:

- Everyone can learn new things (growth mindset belief).
- Some kids are born smarter than others (fixed mindset belief).
- We can change how smart we are (growth mindset belief).

In all of the classrooms that I surveyed (classrooms made up of high-poverty, diverse students, as well as classrooms with students classified primarily as middle-class), 100% percent of the kindergarten children demonstrated growth mindset thinking. They came to school in kindergarten thinking that they could learn and be successful. They were enthusiastic, full of promise, and ready to absorb social and intellectual knowledge!

With that optimistic data in hand, I moved on to first-grade classrooms; again, students were surveyed to capture their thinking about intelligence. In this case, only 10% of students in first-grade classes demonstrated fixed mindset thinking. For the most part, these first graders replicated the enthusiasm of the kindergarten students with the exception of only a few students who felt that some students were born smarter than others and that we cannot really change how smart we are. Time to move on to second grade. In these classrooms, I discovered that 18% of students demonstrated fixed mindset thinking. Are you beginning to see a pattern? With every increase in grade, more and more students believed that intelligence was a fixed trait: They agreed with the notion that "Some people are smart, and some people are not." But perhaps the most surprising result was the large jump between second and third grade. Of the third-grade students I surveyed, 42% demonstrated fixed mindset thinking! Table 1.1 displays these findings.

This data sends a message loud and clear: We need to start working with educators, children, and parents as early as possible so they can maintain a belief system that communicates that all students can succeed. Our children walk into the school

Table 1.1

Changes in Fixed and Growth Mindsets Across Grade Levels

Grade	Fixed Mindset	Growth Mindset
K	n/a	100%
1	10%	90%
2	18%	82%
3	42%	58%

building on the first day of preschool or kindergarten ready to learn, believing in themselves with all of the optimism a four- and five-year-old can muster. We need to capture and sustain that mindset as they make their way through school. Now, how can we accomplish this?

> *On a side note, a 2021 analysis of The Mindset Assessment Profile (which is part of the Mindset Works website: https://www.mindsetworks.com).* Reconsidering the Use of the Mindset Assessment Profile in Educational Contexts *found that "In sum, despite the Mindset Assessment Profile's stated purpose as a mindset assessment and diagnostic tool, our results indicate that it is a poor measure of mindset. We recommend researchers avoid using the Mindset Assessment Profile as a measure of mindset or as a diagnostic tool in educational contexts."* (Burgoyne AP, Macnamara BN. The study can be found here: https://www.ncbi.nlm.nih.gov/pmc/articles/PMC8395928/)

Since the release of the first edition of this book, many educators have approached me and asked if I could identify the most important components of a growth mindset learning environment. In other words, what are the actions that must occur in order to have a growth mindset district, school, or classroom? After much listening, observing, research, and reflection, I have identified four components that are essential to a growth mindset learning culture. These are areas that each learning environment should strive to obtain.

These can't happen overnight and sometimes not even within one school year. These actions should be a long-term commitment, and educators must have a growth mindset themselves in order to persevere to attain these goals. These four components are:

1. Equitable access to advanced learning opportunities
2. Deliberate cultivation of psychosocial skills such as perseverance and resiliency
3. Student understanding of neural networks in the brain
4. Growth mindset feedback and praise

Let's break these four components (also found in Figure 1.1) down a little bit.

Equitable Access to Advanced Learning Opportunities

Do all of the students in your class, school, or district have access to enriched and accelerated learning? Is a label (such as "Gifted" or "TAG"), a grade, or a specific test score a requirement to access these opportunities? Ongoing informal assessment and observation should allow for all students, not just those with already developed abilities, to have access to and participate in advanced learning opportunities. This may be

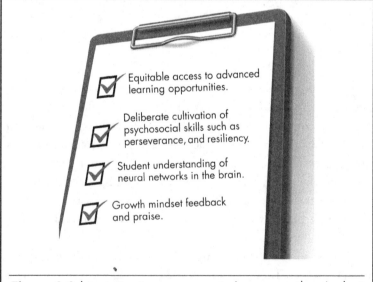

Figure 1.1 Important components in a growth mindset learning environment

teacher-facilitated small-group work within the classroom or an advanced class offering at the secondary level. Teachers must practice growth mindset thinking in order to allow this to happen. No gatekeeping, no barriers, no "sorry, but you are not ready for this." Once students have this access, are supports put in place to help students succeed?

On a visit with a group of high school teachers, they proudly announced that they had open access to all of their Honors and Advanced Placement (AP) courses. Any student who wanted to enroll could enroll. My momentary joy did not last long—they shared that most of those students who self-enroll without the recommendation of a teacher don't "make it" in the class. After some discussion, two things were determined. First, the Honors and AP courses were not at all responsive or differentiated to meet students' needs. The teachers just instructed the whole class as if all of the 25+ kids were on the same level. Second, they possessed a "sink or swim" mentality. The attitude was that if the student was in the class, they should be able to handle it or they don't "deserve" to be in the class. No supports or scaffolds were in place for a student who struggled. In fact, in many cases, the student was counseled to move to a standard-level class at the first sign of struggle. On a side note, struggle (particularly productive struggle) is not necessarily a bad thing. It is actually a good experience for a student to struggle because resiliency cannot be developed without experiencing some degree of struggle. With equitable access, provisions should be in place to help students succeed. As a former district Supervisor for Advanced Academics, the children I lost sleep over were those who were not provided the opportunity to access challenging learning experiences.

Deliberate Cultivation of Psychosocial Skills

The cultivation of noncognitive/psychosocial skills is imperative, for both the students who have not yet developed their abilities and/or talents and for high-performing students.

If I had to choose the most important skills that must be deliberately modeled, taught, and cultivated, I would select perseverance and resiliency.

Development of these psychosocial skills should be part of the climate of the classroom, discussed across every content area, and modeled daily by the entire class or school community. Students can self-evaluate and make plans for improving and tracking their growth in these skills; then they can make a conscious effort to improve their ability to bounce back after a less-than-successful performance or failure to master a new concept. They can begin working toward being diligent about their actions. Hand-in-hand with nurturing perseverance and resiliency is teaching students how to learn from errors and failure. Mistakes should be considered "data"—this data can help a student set goals for moving toward success.

A recommended first step in deliberate cultivation of psychosocial skills is to reflect upon what is already in place in your classroom or school. Focus on areas that overlap at first, such as perseverance and resiliency, and then gather some interested staff members. Together, brainstorm school or districtwide experiences that will deliberately cultivate these noncognitive factors. Establish Look-Fors and a plan for monitoring (not grading) student progress over time in the areas of concentration. Take a look at Table 1.2, Schoolwide Psychosocial Skills Reflection; this is a sample of one way to capture what your classroom or school is already doing as well as a place to brainstorm ideas about what you can do to further these. This can be used individually, with content-area or grade-level teams, or schoolwide.

Some schools have developed transition courses for students entering middle school (sixth grade) or high school (ninth grade). These courses provide sixth graders or freshmen an opportunity to focus on those important elements that will help them be successful. Study skills, how to cultivate healthy relationships with their peers, as well as a big focus on the growth mindset principles of perseverance and resilience, are all

Table 1.2
Schoolwide Psychosocial Skills Reflection

Psychosocial skill (noncognitive)	Practices in place that cultivate the skill	Ideas that would further develop the skill	Ideas for measuring progress in this area
Perseverance	Students and teachers/support staff who go above and beyond in demonstrating perseverance are recognized with a shout-out on morning announcements.	School counselors or student advisors will do weekly growth mindset lessons focusing on perseverance and resiliency. Schoolwide assemblies could focus on perseverance. Grade-level or content-area teams will identify a video or a piece of text to use each week that will elicit a discussion about perseverance, resiliency, or growth mindset.	Students will self-evaluate each quarter using a district or school-created electronic survey. Teachers will identify a few students who give up easily and maintain anecdotal records that will capture their growth.
Resiliency	None (yet!)	Students and teachers/support staff who go above and beyond in demonstrating resiliency will be recognized with a shout-out on morning announcements.	Students will self-evaluate each quarter using a district- or school-created electronic survey.

emphasized. The teachers of these courses also encourage their students to embrace challenges through growth mindset thinking. Additionally, many of these courses provide opportunities to deliberately practice strategies that students can use when they get stuck on a task. (See page 24 for an explanation of these strategies.)

Building a Conceptual Understanding of the Brain and Neural Networks

Having an understanding of neural networking can significantly increase motivation. In Carol Dweck's (2006) original New York City study, students reported that visualizing neural connections helped them move forward. In my visits to schools, I have often heard students state that they think about the neurons connecting when they are faced with a difficult task or have difficulty understanding a new skill or concept. This does not require going deep into neuroscience—just building a conceptual understanding can increase motivation to succeed.

Growth Mindset Feedback and Praise

Strive for a learning space that praises effort, struggle, and perseverance. Provide feedback and praise when students select difficult tasks to conquer or try new strategies when learning a concept. This feedback also encompasses how you react to student behavior, such as a typically strong student not having success on an assessment.

The learning environment, whether it is a classroom, field, court, in front of a piano, or at the kitchen table, should be a setting where both adults and students favor the word "*yet*": "You are not quite there…yet…with more practice, you will be."

Keep the power of the word "yet" in mind as you embark on creating a growth mindset world for your students. The next chapter provides guidance for beginning this journey.

GROWTH MINDSETS IN STUDENTS
WHO LIVE IN POVERTY

Stanford University researchers conducted powerful research that has implications for high-poverty schools and districts. The study looked at the mindsets of 10th-grade high school students who lived in poverty. Researchers found that students living in poverty achieved at a lower level and were more likely to demonstrate fixed mindset thinking—this is not a surprising finding. What is a hopeful finding is that researchers found that students living in poverty who did have a growth mindset achieved at a higher level. In some cases, in this group of growth mindset thinkers, their measures of achievement were equal to those of middle-class students. This study suggests that high-poverty schools could benefit by adopting a growth mindset learning environment (Yirka, 2016). The following chapters will provide guidance for doing just that!

At this point, some of you may be thinking about whether the effectiveness of Growth Mindset is valid. After all, there have been some studies that suggest that growth mindset does not have an impact on student achievement after interventions have been put in place. That brings me to my first point: I am not recommending a specific intervention program—no growth mindset computer program, workbook, or set of lesson plans will have a huge impact on a lot of students at a variety of grade levels. Rather, embed the principles of growth mindset into your everyday curriculum and instruction (there are some Reading Language Arts and Math textbook teacher editions that deliberately included suggestions about ways to embed Growth Mindset). The second point is that many of these studies are flawed—with a one and done lesson as an intervention, a small group of students, and/or only one grade level without a diverse learner group.

If you are interested in a summary of some of the research, Cognitive Scientist, Daniel Willingham, shares a good summary in this article, *Ask a Cognitive Scientist: Does Developing a Growth Mindset Help Students Learn?*, specifically Willingham reviews research and comes to the conclusion that "There's good evidence for the psychological validity of the theory and that the theory can be used to help students".

Additionally, Trevor Ragan and David Yeager summarize some of the research and introduce the notion of a stress mindset on the video, *The New Era of Growth Mindset* https://www.youtube.com/watch?v =FLD01N0IQIM.

In *How the Brain Learns* (2022), David Sousa shares that teachers play a significant role in helping students who engage in fixed mindset thinking transform into growth mindset thinkers. He shares this summary of an article from the *Journal of Applied Developmental Psychology*.

> Studies reveal that teachers with growth mindsets have a positive and statistically significant association with the development of their students' growth mindsets, particularly for boys. (Mesler et al., 2021)

We all take our role as educators seriously and can feel overwhelmed with curriculum changes, safety protocols, helping students fill in the gaps from learning loss due to the pandemic, and more. The good news is that growth mindset thinking is not about unpacking and learning a new curriculum or analyzing test data— it's about how we view ourselves and how we view our students— through a lens of potential and possibilities.

References

Burgoyne, A. P., & Macnamara, B. N. (2021, August 4). Reconsidering the use of the mindset assessment profile in educational contexts. *Journal of Intelligence*, 9(3), 39. https://

doi.org/10.3390/jintelligence9030039. PMID: 34449686; PMCID: PMC8395928.

Dweck, C. S. (2006). *Mindset: The new psychology of success.* New York: Random House.

Mesler, R. M., Corbin, C. M., & Martin, B. H. (2021, July–September). Teacher mindset is associated with development of students' growth mindset. *Journal of Applied Development Psychology, 76,* 101299.

Olszewski-Kubilius, P. (2013, October). Talent development as an emerging framework for gifted education. Presentation given to Baltimore County Public Schools, MD.

Palmer, B. (2011). How can you increase your IQ? *Slate.* Retrieved from http://www.slate.com/articles/news_and_politics/explainer/2011/10/increasing_your_iq.html.

Ricci, M. C., & Lee, M. (2024). *Mindsets for parents: Strategies to encourage growth mindsets in Kids* (2nd ed.). Routledge.

Sousa, D. A. (2022). *How the brain learns,* 6th ed. Thousand Oaks, CA: Corwin, a Sage Publishing Company.

Willingham, D. T. (Winter 2022–2023). Ask the cognitive scientist: Does developing a growth mindset help students learn? *American Educator.* Retrieved from https://www.aft.org/ae/winter2022-2023/willingham.

Yirka, B. (2016). Growth mindset found to temper impact of poverty on student achievement. *Phys.org.* Retrieved from https://phys.org/news/2016-07-growth-mindset-temper-impact-poverty.html.

CHAPTER 2

WHAT ARE SOME WAYS TO BEGIN BUILDING A GROWTH MINDSET SCHOOL CULTURE?

"I can learn and get smarter even when work is hard."–Grade 4 student

Before getting into the how-to, let's highlight some of the challenges that I have observed in schools and classrooms as educators begin to build a growth mindset environment. One of the biggest barriers toward a growth mindset environment that I have observed has been well-meaning educators who continually communicate messages that tell students that they can be successful—all they have to do is stick with it and try hard. So, what is wrong with this message? It is about what is missing from this message—we must first make sure that our students have the strategies or tools that they need to have success. If students do not, they may continue to try again and again in the same way with the same result.

DOI: 10.4324/9781003406914-2

What is a typical action from a teacher who notices that a student is struggling with a concept or task? To help, of course! As educators, we all tend to sometimes "rescue" students a little too quickly from their struggle. The reason is twofold: first, we want to help, but second, it also is the quickest way to get students back on task.

In a growth mindset learning environment, students must first learn (1) how to use a variety of strategies to learn and (2) how to ask for specific help when those strategies are not working. The strategies that our students need to implement are similar to many of the strategies you use when you are teaching a new skill or concept.

What do your students do when they are stuck? Do they have some practiced strategies that they keep in their back pocket? Here are a few of the more generic (not content or grade level-specific) strategies that they can use:

- **Think aloud or self-talk** (metacognition)
  Did you ever find yourself explaining an issue to a colleague, friend, or partner when right in the middle of a sentence, you find yourself saying, "Oh, never mind, I know what to do"? The act of explaining the situation aloud actually helped you think it through and understand the issue. This is what "think aloud" or "self-talk" does for students.

- **Breaking material down into smaller chunks**
  We know how to do this for our students, but do students know how to do this for themselves?
  Did you ever feel overwhelmed and not know where to begin? Perhaps your home organization has gotten away from you and you don't have the motivation to begin because it feels like an impossible task. You need to break it down into manageable chunks. Perhaps one room at a time, or a corner of that room, or a closet or if things are really overwhelming…you may need to begin with a shelf. We know how to do this—but we need to teach our students how to take a big task and make it more manageable.

- **Taking a break——increases productivity and creativity**
  A short break (5–8 minutes) has the ability to refresh our brains and may help students find a solution that they previously didn't see.

  This works with adults as well—like many of you, I enjoy playing games on my phone or tablet to keep my brain stimulated. I especially enjoy word games where you are given specific letters and have to create words from them. Often, I will leave the game and come back later and easily see some words that I did not see prior to the break. This break gave my brain a chance to refresh and process information.

- **Review previous feedback or examples**
  Deliberately teach our students to look at past work, read the comments that you have provided, and check online and paper resources for examples. When reviewing this strategy with students, allow time for them to practice doing this with your feedback.

- **Highlight to help focus**
  Highlighting does not just mean using a highlighter or a highlight feature on a laptop or tablet. Highlighting can include a plethora of options: from creating a window in an index card or on a tablet/laptop to focus on important text to using a small flashlight to zero in on words and phrases. (Little ones love this one.)

- **Ask for help with a *specific* question** (*after* they have tried some strategies)
  "I don't get this" or "I need help" does not allow a student to engage in the content before asking for help. Require students to state something, anything that they understand about the task before asking a question. Otherwise, they may jump right into asking for help before engaging in the task to take the easy way out.

The first stop along the path to building a growth mindset culture is to begin to build a school culture that values intellectual growth with a staff who have internalized the belief that intelligence can be cultivated. Ideally, every adult in the building must work toward adopting a mindset where he or she believes that with effort, motivation, perseverance, and the right menu of teaching strategies, all students can achieve great things. School secretaries, building service workers, classroom paraeducators/aides, as well as teachers and administrators, should all commit to contributing to a growth mindset school climate.

Professional learning sessions for all school personnel are the initial step toward this goal. If you are a member of your school Leadership Team, an instructional coach, or a staff member who values growth mindset principles, collaboratively plan professional learning sessions for your school. It is important to first determine what belief systems are held by staff at the present time. Whether you are working independently toward this goal or with a grade-level team, an entire staff, or the school system, it is important to begin by reflecting on your own personal belief system regarding intelligence. Suggestions for professional development can be found on the following pages.

Step 1: Reflect and Preassess

Prior to a series of professional development sessions, teachers from a high-poverty, urban school district on the East Coast were asked to write down what they believed about intelligence using the form in Figure 2.1.

These teachers' classrooms ranged from preschool through high school, with a wide spectrum of experience in education. Responses were varied and revealed many different opinions about intelligence. Teachers whose responses demonstrated fixed mindset thinking had responses like the following:

- "Intelligence is something you are born with (or not), and it's an unchangeable part of you."

- "It is innate and hereditary."
- "Intelligence does not change much throughout the lifetime; IQ stays roughly the same from age 8."
- "Intelligence is a student's ability to intake information, retain it, and regurgitate it at any given time."

Collecting and analyzing these responses served as a preassessment for me as I planned for professional learning sessions; the goal was to capture their thinking prior to a series of workshops promoting malleable intelligence and then ask them to respond to the same question at the end of the workshop series. (Preassessment also models the first step required in planning for differentiated instruction, which will be addressed more completely in the next chapter.) I found that roughly one third of these teachers demonstrated a mindset where they believed that intelligence can be developed and two thirds held a belief that intelligence is fixed and stagnant, just like those quoted above. Interestingly, no pattern existed among the age or grade level of the students they taught; however, slightly more of the less-experienced teachers tended to hold growth

---

Please share your beliefs about intelligence and/or what you were taught about student intelligence as you prepared to become a teacher.

My beliefs about intelligence are:

_____
_____
_____
_____
_____

Upon completion, put this in an envelope and put your name and today's date on the front of the envelope.

Later in the year, open the envelope and look at the response you wrote today. Reflect on any changes in your response.

Figure 2.1 Teacher reflection about intelligence prior to professional learning sessions

mindset thinking, while the more experienced teachers held fixed mindset thinking. (This difference also may have been due to when they completed their teaching degree coupled with neuroscience beliefs at that time. Perhaps the more-experienced teachers finished their degrees during the time when the "bell curve" mentality was more present and widely ascribed to in teacher education; this theory purported that there would always be students who were at the low end who could only go so far.)

A similar process can be conducted in your own school to see how your teachers feel about intelligence. Ideally, teachers should reflect and respond to the statement, "My beliefs about intelligence are..." privately, seal their responses in an envelope, and at the end of the professional learning series, compare their present mindset to their initial one.

After these individual reflections are complete, ask the staff members if they agree or disagree with the following statements that were adapted from Carol Dweck's (2006) work:

- Our intelligence is one of our basic traits.
- We can all learn new things, but we cannot really change how smart we are.

Assess the responses to see who agrees or disagrees with these statements. Educators might agree with both of these statements if they were taught or were raised to believe that intelligence cannot change.

Step 2: Educate Staff About the Malleability of the Brain

Some educators will resist the belief that all students can master high standards and that "gifted" behaviors can be developed. As I mentioned previously, this can be due in large part to how the teachers and administrators have been educated. Some college and university teacher prep programs supported the bell curve mentality of intelligence. Future teachers learned that a typical classroom will contain students at the "top," in the "middle," and at the "bottom." Does that always have to be the case? Can all students reach mastery? Can all students exceed grade-level expectations? Not everyone can be a Maya Angelou, Steve Jobs, Oprah Winfrey, or Nelson Mandela, but these people did not become who they were without much practice, effort, perseverance, and work ethic.

Using the data you collected from Step 1, begin to plan ways to educate staff about theories of malleable intelligence. It is important to be aware that this will be a very new way of thinking for some educators, so be sensitive in the delivery of the message. Remember, many people believe that intelligence is an innate, permanent attribute that we are born with.

One analogy that can be made when communicating this change of thinking is to ask teachers to think about how a toothache is treated. Fifty years ago, when someone had a terrible toothache, how was it treated? Most likely, the tooth was pulled. Today, because of advanced learning in the field of dentistry as well as new technological possibilities, more options are available. It is important to use examples such as this to give educators an "out" when learning about the possibilities of cultivating intelligence.

In Guy Kawasaki's book, *Enchantment: The Art of Changing Hearts, Minds, and Actions* (Kawasaki 2011), he describes two kinds of people in the world:

> Eaters and bakers. Eaters want a bigger slice of an existing pie; bakers want to make a bigger pie. Eaters think that if they win, you lose, and if you win, they lose. Bakers think that everyone can live with a bigger pie. (p. 33)

Just like the bakers, all students can win without the existence of "losers" in the class. The "bigger pie" in this case is a growth mindset culture in the classroom.

It has been my experience that some teachers may feel a level of guilt after learning that intelligence can be developed. In the past, these teachers may have grouped and instructed students according to perceived intelligence or lowered expectations for some children for the same reason. Let educators know that it is because of new studies and scientific brain research that we now think differently about children and their potential, so they should not feel badly about past practices. Instead, they can and should look forward—a growth mindset can be cultivated and shifted from a fixed belief.

Using the information that you learned from your preassessment, collaboratively plan multiple professional development sessions over several months. Share recent research about developed intelligence as well as the outcomes and educational implications based on the research. Using Dweck's (2006) terms of "fixed" and "growth" is entirely up to the individual school or district. You can also refer to the concepts as malleable, developed, or flexible intelligence (growth) or static, stationary, or stagnant intelligence (fixed). Some schools chose to adopt a school motto: "We can all get smart at Harmony Park," or "Our Effort Is the Best at Havencrest." Understanding conceptually and communicating that intelligence is not a stagnant, innate attribute is the most important aspect of professional learning sessions. It is not important what specific researcher, book, or study this idea is built upon. The important thing is to just get the conversation started! One way to get staff thinking about this concept is by asking a few of the following discussion questions:

- Do we, as a society, believe in or demonstrate a growth mindset? Why or why not?
- In what areas, personal or professional, do you have a fixed mindset? Why?

Many teachers have cited the following examples as areas in which they have a fixed mindset about their weaknesses or areas that they "will never be good at": technology, cooking, managing finances, sports. After teachers share some of the areas where they may have a fixed mindset, pose this question: "If you were given appropriate instruction, learned successful strategies, and you had the time, persistence, and motivation, could you become a better cook? Money manager? Pickleball player?" (Most will respond with a resounding "yes"). Then ask, "What if you wanted to learn to sing like Michael Bublé or Beyonce? Well, you may or may not reach that goal, but with the proper instruction, much practice and effort, as well as motivation, could you become a better singer?" Yes! Most of us hold a fixed mindset in some aspects of our lives, and so we sit on a continuum between "Of course I can do that!" and "I could never do that!" Providing everyday examples like these helps educators apply the concepts of malleable intelligence more easily.

Another way to introduce teachers to the idea of mindset is to talk about how one's emotions can be changed based on one's thinking, attitude, and behaviors. Andrew Weil, a doctor and author of the book *Spontaneous Happiness: A New Path to Emotional Well-Being* (Weil, 2011), pointed to studies that show not only that intelligence can be developed, but emotions such as happiness and empathy can be developed as well. In the same way that practice improves a singer's voice, an athlete's performance, or a mathematician's growth and development, practice can also help a person become happier. Weil cited studies of the brain organized by Richard Davidson, Director of the Laboratory for Affective Neuroscience at the University of Wisconsin-Madison. Davidson performed brain scans on Matthieu Ricard, a Frenchman who attained a doctorate in molecular genetics, then later became a Buddhist monk. Based on data collection Davidson completed, he dubbed Ricard "The World's Happiest Man." What he found was that Ricard had increased activity in the left prefrontal cortex, which is associated with positive emotions. Ricard makes an effort to be happy, practices happiness, and works to eliminate negative emotions through meditation—remember, he is now a Buddhist monk! This study demonstrates that happiness can be learned with specific practice and effort.

Being an optimistic learner is beneficial for students, as it helps them become ready to master new learning and be optimistic about their ability to do so. Remember Chapter 1's discussion of neuroplasticity? It is because of the brain's neuroplasticity that we have the ability to become happier.

Step 3: Educate Staff About Praising Students

How do we praise our students? Walking through almost any school, you can hear teachers praising student success, behaviors, and attitudes. We need to be more aware of the way we praise students if we are journeying down the path of a growth mindset school culture. Carol Dweck and her colleagues have presented sound evidence about the value of praising effort rather than outcome. Dweck (2006) has discovered through her research that students who believe that intelligence is something you are born with and cannot change are overly concerned about looking smart. This is particularly true with gifted and highly able students.

Therefore, praise such as "You are so smart" could be detrimental for students who hold a fixed belief about intelligence. Saying "You are so smart" is the equivalent of saying "You are so tall"— what did a child have to do with being tall? It is just a genetic trait that the child had no control over. Both statements recognize no action that the child has put forth. No effort is recognized. When adults praise what a child "is," such as tall or smart, the children attribute their accomplishment to a fixed trait they were born with. When adults praise actions or tasks that children "do," the children attribute accomplishment to their own effort. Often it is just a matter of adding on to the praise that is already stated. For example, if a teacher says, "You did a great job on that paper," she might add, "I can tell you worked very hard." Modifying or adding effort praise is all it takes to send a growth mindset message. Adults must also be aware of the nonverbal messages that they are sending to students. Folded arms, a stern face, a heavy sigh, or a roll of the eyes do not send a growth mindset message, no matter what words are coming from a person.

It is important to note that some gifted and highly able students believe that putting forth a lot of effort is a sign of weakness. If they have constantly been told that they are "gifted" and/or smart, they think that learning should be easy for them; therefore, they think that if you have to work hard, you must not be smart.

Schools should provide professional learning sessions for all adults in the building that focus on ways to praise students who value and promote growth. It is also important to put in place a support system that can provide feedback to staff. Peer coaching or school leadership can provide constructive feedback to all staff. Adjusting feedback and praise is not as easy as it may sound—be purposeful with what is said to students and patient with yourself as you work toward growth mindset praise and feedback. I highly recommend the five-minute video, "Carol Dweck: A Study on Praise and Mindsets." (It should be shown and discussed at a staff meeting in every school!) It is a wonderful synthesis of Dweck's research about praise. It can be found here: https://www.youtube.com/watch?v=NWv1VdDeoRY

Step 4: Educate Teachers
Learning and the Brain

Although happening more often over the past few years, it is still somewhat rare for me to run into an educator who has had coursework or has independently read about the brain and its implications for learning. This goes back to that first question we asked educators to reflect on, "What is intelligence?" Many educators think they know enough about the brain. They may think that some children's brains are "quicker" and others "slower." The truth is that neuroscience is a field that is constantly changing, and keeping up with all of the studies and research requires a commitment. Even though the field of neuroscience is complex, basic conceptual understanding of the brain is simple and important for teachers as well as students.

In a nutshell: neurons (brain cells) make new connections when you learn something new. These connections become stronger with practice and effort. The more connections, the denser your brain is. The more density, the "smarter" you are. Educators and students should have a clear understanding that these neural connections or pathways become stronger every time they are used. Picture brand new learning experiences as neurons being connected by a thin piece of thread. Every time that new learning is practiced and applied, that thin thread becomes stronger and stronger until the learning is mastered. Once we really understand what was once new knowledge, that weak, thin piece of thread will then have the strength of a thick, strong rope. In order to strengthen these neural connections for students, it is important for teachers to consistently make connections to prior knowledge and experiences. The more connections that are made during a learning sequence, the more physical changes occur in the brain by developing and strengthening neural pathways. (Sample learning tasks for students can be found in Chapter 8.)

Another way to look at it is to picture a new neural pathway as if you are walking through an unexplored forest for the first time. The more frequently the path is used, the fewer the barriers and obstacles that stand in the way. Eventually, a clear path is created. That new path represents a clear understanding of the content being taught.

Step 5: Teach Students About the Brain

Neuroscience is not a typical area of study in elementary and middle school curriculum, and with the exception of a chapter or unit embedded in biology or psychology classes, it is not often found in high school science. So how do educators find the time to teach students about their brain? The content needs to be revisited often and built upon over time. It is about introducing and explicitly teaching students, then routinely revisiting the concept of malleable intelligence so that students realize that intelligence is not about a fixed number, a grade on a paper, or a report card. Learners must understand that intelligence is constantly changing based on effort, perseverance, practice, and the struggle that they experience. They will soon realize that intelligence is something that grows as you use it and declines if you don't.

More and more studies are surfacing about the importance of teaching neuroscience. A study titled, *Young Children's Changing Conceptualizations of Brain Function: Implications for Teaching Neuroscience in Early Elementary Settings* (Marshall & Comalli, 2012) consisted of a two-part study of children ages 4–14. The goal of the first part of the study was to determine what exactly these children already knew about the brain. The results indicated that the vast majority of these children believed that the brain's functions are limited to intellectual activity. In other words, they believed it is strictly used for thinking. Based on these results, a second study was conducted that determined that this very narrow view of brain function could be broadened with classroom instruction. In this case, lessons were designed to teach kids about the brain's broader involvement with their five senses, physical activity, and everyday actions. This study found that with classroom lessons, first-grade students became significantly more aware of their brain's involvement with all of their senses rather than maintaining the narrow view of "My brain helps me think."

Step 6: Educate Parents

When providing workshops for parents on the topic of malleable intelligence and growth mindset, I have found that it is often a wake-up call for many of the parents I work with when the discussion of the importance of having a growth mindset and not looking at their children through a lens of perceived intelligence takes place. At the conclusion of these parent workshops, I take a few moments and ask parents to reflect on what they just heard. They are asked to jot down what they are thinking and what they are planning as a result of the presentation. Many are reflective about the way they speak to their kids. For example, one parent shared:

I am planning on starting to make changes tomorrow morning during "morning rush." Instead of saying, "You're so slow" or "You're such a slowpoke," I will say "I really appreciate the effort that you put forth to get to school on time." I need to make a lot of changes.

It is also interesting to note that in almost every workshop, a parent asks, "Well, do the teachers know about this?" Parent associations can also sponsor book clubs using *Mindsets for Parents: Strategies to Encourage Growth Mindset in Kids* (updated in 2024), which serves as a partner book to this one. It is also available in Spanish for Spanish-speaking families in the community. More ideas for parents can be found in Chapter 6.

The Final Step: Monitor and Review School Protocols

If you are in a position where you have spent a good amount of time and effort toward building a growth mindset culture, then it is now time to evaluate how well you, your school, or your district is doing. How do you monitor and make sure that, in fact, the building staff is working toward this every day? One way is to establish "Look Fors", student and teacher behaviors that you will observe when you walk through any room in the school building. These behaviors should evidence the focus on growth in your building (sample Look Fors can be found in Chapter 9). Another option is to utilize Professional Learning Communities (PLCs) or Networks (PLNs). These groups should focus discussion around the progress toward a growth mindset culture. Set up alerts online so leaders of PLCs will be notified when new articles or studies are released that focus on neuroscience in education and growth mindset. Have the PLCs adopt books like this one or other titles as book studies or book club selections. Reflecting on these readings together will help internalize the concept of mindsets.

Think about how students are placed in instructional groups and classes. Does the current student placement system contribute to a growth mindset culture within the school? Do all students have equitable access to advanced learning opportunities? The following is an actual exchange of e-mails between a parent of an incoming ninth-grade student and the English department chair at the student's receiving high school. Read this exchange through the lens of a growth mindset (Names and specific details have been changed).

Dear English Department Chair,

We are thrilled that our daughter, Emma, will be attending Great Hills High School next year. We wanted to share with you some information about her interest in literature. During her eighth-grade year, her love of literature has exploded! This is due, in part, to a great literature experience she has had this year. We have seen Emma dive deeply into the symbolism of each book she reads—she asks questions, interprets, analyzes characters' words and actions, foreshadows, and wants to discuss each and every book that she reads. Her writing has also shown great improvement over the last few months. We are thrilled about her passion for literature. Standardized testing does not reflect this surge of interest, motivation, and achievement in the area of reading with meaningful interpretation. We are wondering what steps need to be taken in order to have her placed in freshman-level Honors literature. She has maintained an A in Reading so far this year.

Emma has adopted a strong growth mindset in the area of literature, and she feels strongly that she can succeed in an Honors literature class. We obviously do not want to see this growth and enthusiasm diminish in her. Please let us know what the process is for making this request. Thank you for your time and we look forward to hearing from you.

Sincerely,
Mr. and Mrs. M

The response to the parents:

Dear Mr. and Mrs. M,

Thank you so much for your recent inquiry as to the feasibility of effecting a class placement change for your daughter, Emma. Placement is determined by the department chairs and in some cases consultation with other school staff. It is based on the candidate's performance on the placement test. We do take into consideration the candidate's grades in English and Reading as well (when a candidate is on the cusp of our cut-off criteria), but given the varied levels of preparedness of students coming from many different feeder schools, the scores do offer us the best method of determining the appropriate placement of the incoming students. The cut-off for Honors placement is as follows: 75 (verbal skills), 75 (reading). Your daughter's scores are far below the minimum cut-off. Please also understand that we have a large number of students who score well above this bar. You mentioned that she received an A in Reading, but also that this interest just surfaced during eighth grade, which brings into question the level of preparedness.

Although I understand that you do not wish to witness her recent interest in literature wane, I would like to emphasize that our standard freshmen English classes are rigorous enough to challenge our students. She will be challenged in a Standard English class freshman year, where we would be able to fill in any gaps and afford her the opportunity to develop a solid foundation of not only critical reading, but also analytical writing. If she earns an A in standard college prep English freshman year, she will be moved into honors English sophomore year.

Kind regards,
Department Chair–English

First the good news: the department chair wrote a response that addressed most of the points that the parents brought up in the letter. Emma's parents asked for information about the process for requesting a specific class placement, and the response back basically stated that no process existed for parents to make this request. Technically, the school response was a well-thought-out, well-written letter. However, those of you who are well on your way to adopting a growth mindset and read it through a growth mindset lens probably need to take a deep breath. I know I had to when I read this response. This kind of gatekeeping occurs through all grade levels in many schools. Emma is demonstrating enthusiasm, motivation, and willingness to welcome the challenge of an honors-level course. The department chair is demonstrating a fixed mindset, a belief that this child does not have the innate ability to handle an honors-level course based on a multicontent placement test given one morning of this child's life. If you analyze the response further, she also points out to the parents that the child fell "far below" their "cut-off." (Message to parents: "Your child is not smart.") If your class placement process even entertains the words "cut-off," then the process is not one that truly contributes to a growth mindset culture. Look at the response again and keep an eye out for other statements that scream, "Your child can't handle this." The fact that the incoming student is referred to as a "candidate" also sends a message. Synonyms for "candidate" include contender, nominee, and contestant; the child simply wants to enroll in an honors class, not run for a political office. Also keep in mind that the decision to keep this child out of the course that she has the motivation to take was made without ever having met her. If the school or staff member was not willing to let the child into an honors-level course based on a test score, perhaps inviting the child in for an informal discussion about a book she has read and to gauge her motivation would have been an appropriate intermediate step that could have occurred. The way this situation played out is a clear example of gatekeeping and a fixed mindset mentality.

Sharing the above communication or one like it (perhaps from your own school or district) with staff can actually be an effective way to initiate a deep discussion with your team or staff about beliefs and school policies. Some educators may see nothing wrong with the above decision. If this is the case, challenge them to view it again through the lens of a fixed or growth mindset. What message does this send to a child? If a student has the motivation, resiliency, and willingness to put forth the effort, is she allowed opportunities to be engaged in higher level classes in your school or district? Monitoring how teachers interact with students and communicate growth mindset messages is only part of the process. Evaluating current instructional practices and policies within the school or district is also imperative.

So what happened to Emma when she was kept out of the honors-level class? Well, sadly, Emma no longer has a great enthusiasm for literature. There are probably several reasons why this occurred, the first being that she was not with a peer group in her English class who shared her enthusiasm for literature. Interpretive discussions were scant, differentiation did not occur, and she began to believe that, well, maybe English was not her thing after all. Another contributor was that solid classroom management did not exist yet, and instructional time was used to get students in line and ready to learn. Although she was with a first-year teacher who showed great potential, management was not yet a strength. Content that was part of the freshmen English class was "covered," but the instruction lacked depth. Writing was not explicitly taught based on student strengths or needs, and when the parent asked for clarity about writing instruction, she was told (by the same department chair) that students were expected to know how to write well when they entered high school.

Suffice it to say that due to the school's and/or educator's fixed mindset and gatekeeping practices, a child who was ready to embrace a challenge and be successful now believes that she cannot do so. If policymakers at Emma's school were educated and believed in neuroscience studies that demonstrate the plasticity of the brain and the value of motivation, perhaps Emma could have developed her love of literature.

References

Dweck, C. (2006). Carol Dweck and her colleagues have presented sound evidence about the value of praising effort rather than outcome.

Kawasaki, G. (2011). *Enchantment: The art of changing hearts, minds, and actions*. New York: Portfolio/Penguin.

Marshall, P., & Comalli, C. (2012). Young children's changing conceptualizations of brain function: Implications for teaching neuroscience in early elementary settings. *Early Education and Development, 23*(1), 4–23.

Weil, A. (2011). *Spontaneous happiness: A new path to emotional well-being*. New York: Little, Brown.

CHAPTER 3

WHY IS A DIFFERENTIATED, RESPONSIVE CLASSROOM IMPORTANT FOR A GROWTH MINDSET CULTURE?

"My brain is getting smarter and smarter each day."—Grade 1 student

The mindset of a teacher contributes greatly to his or her responsiveness to the needs of students. If an educator views a child through a deficit lens, then that child will not be given opportunities to grow unless he or she is in a responsive classroom. Deficit thinking is a practice of making assumptions about a child's ability based on perceived deficits or because of race, low-income status, English language acquisition, or a variety of other factors. Educators who value differentiated instruction need to be very aware of the beliefs they hold deep

DOI: 10.4324/9781003406914-3

within themselves regarding student intelligence. I would argue that it is not possible to plan and facilitate an effective, differentiated, responsive classroom if an educator does not really possess the belief that intelligence can develop. Differentiation is responsive instruction. Ask five teachers what "differentiation" means to them, and you are likely to get five different responses. To put it simply, differentiation is the way a teacher responds to a student's needs.

Differentiation

the way a teacher responds to a student's needs so that each student is challenged at the appropriate level

Let's make an assumption that you work hard to practice growth mindset thinking and want to be responsive to the potential in all of your students. Many of you know how to effectively differentiate/be responsive to the needs of your students. What instructional structures are in place to guarantee a responsive learning environment? That seems to be the predicament that many teachers face. Once again, we find many new teachers graduate with a teaching degree without having even one class or professional learning session on differentiation or responsive teaching. The focus of this chapter delineates the necessary steps to have a responsive, differentiated classroom.

Preview and Preassess

The initial stage of differentiation involves preassessment, or finding out what students know about a particular skill, concept, or topic before planning for instruction. Preassessment is the first step to creating a differentiated classroom.

In the past, preassessment has been used for years in one particular subject area. Any guesses? Spelling! Historically, students have been given a spelling pretest on Monday and a post-test on Friday. What instructional changes occurred due to the range of outcomes indicated from the spelling pretest? Well, in some classrooms, teachers provided students with different spelling words to learn that were perhaps taken from their own writing. In other classrooms, the "reward" for knowing the words on Monday was more words! So these spellers who showed mastery on the pretest, got to do 30 words instead of 20! (What???) Other times, students just took the pretest, and regardless of what level of mastery was demonstrated, the whole class did the same spelling activities for the week and all took the same test on Friday. As this predicament shows, differentiation and a responsive classroom is not just about administering a preassessment; it is about reflecting and responding to the results.

> ## Preassessment
>
> finding out what students know about a particular skill, concept, or topic before planning for instruction

Preview the Content

It is imperative to learn and respect what students already bring to the classroom. However, before jumping into developing your own or using a ready-made preassessment, an important precursor must take place. You must allow students the opportunity to first "preview" the content being assessed. I know what some of you are thinking: "If I do that, it will be too easy" or "That's cheating!" Not so. In fact, previewing provides an opportunity for students to activate background knowledge and previous learning prior to a preassessment so that the results will be a better reflection of what they understand. It's a way of priming the brain before capturing data that reflects understanding. Imagine that you're getting ready to sit down and read a new book. About five or ten minutes into the story, something is triggered in your mind and you begin to think that perhaps you have read this book before. It starts feeling familiar to you, but the title did not ring a bell. Or maybe, you pick up the book at the library or bookstore and read the blurb on the back cover, and after doing so, remember that you have read it. That blurb activated background knowledge for you; it triggered your memory and served as a preview to the book. It is then that you have an "Aha!" moment and better recall the content of the book.

Previewing should not be a long, drawn-out lesson: five minutes or less is usually enough time to activate prior knowledge. A preview could be as simple as telling students, "Today I would like to see what you know about rounding numbers. Let me show you a few first." Then, proceed to do a few examples on the board. The word "rounding" on a preassessment may not be familiar or trigger any past learning, but after that quick warm-up, lots of students will remember and be ready to show what they know about rounding. Other ways to preview include questioning, watching a short video, interpreting a picture, and listening to a poem or short story with discussion. It can be anything that will trigger previous learning on a topic. What is interesting is that sometimes a preview is all that some students might need to learn a new skill or concept at a basic level.

The impact of previewing before preassessment became very clear for one sixth-grade English teacher. She was preparing a preassessment on figurative language for two different sections of sixth-grade English. This teacher knew that students were introduced to these literary devices around grade 3—the questions were (1) do the students remember the devices, and (2) if they do remember, can that knowledge be applied to a piece of grade-level text?

For one of her classes, she showed a three-minute animated video that she found online. This video was shown prior to the preassessment and reviewed common devices used in figurative language: simile, metaphor, and personification. After viewing the video, she then asked her class to complete a paper-and-pencil preassessment requiring students to identify those devices within a text selection and then write examples of various types of figurative language. She gave two sections of her classes the same preassessment but only previewed the material with one section. The results showed a much higher level of understanding for the students who previewed the material first. In fact, almost half of the previewed class showed complete understanding based upon the preassessment! Only a few students in the class who took the preassessment cold (with no preview) showed understanding of the concept. It is possible that a few of the students learned about similes, metaphors, and personification during that three-minute video (and if they did, and were able to apply that understanding on a preassessment, that gives us good information as well!), but for the majority of students, the preview helped to simply "wake up" the prior learning in their minds.

Developing Preassessments

The effective use of preassessment is essential to ensuring that students and teachers both work from a growth mindset, believing that effort is one of the most important attributes that determines success. Without the use of preassessment, some students do not develop a good work ethic due to the fact that they are "learning" content that they already understand. Even though formative assessments can be used to help determine differentiation during the course of an instructional sequence, preassessments allow for front-end differentiation (we tend to differentiate for students who understand quickly at the end of a unit). Front-end differentiation allows teachers to plan for valuable enrichment and can also provide an opportunity for students to accelerate within the content topic at the beginning of a learning sequence. Preassessment respects a student's time and prior knowledge.

Deciding what kind of preassessment to use depends upon the content being assessed. Preassessments do not always have to be paper-and-pencil tests. For example, in the primary grades you might ask students to demonstrate their knowledge using concrete math manipulatives or by conducting a structured discussion capturing understanding with anecdotal records or from teacher's notes. If you want to assess their knowledge of measurement, then hand them a ruler and see what they can do. In trying to have students recognize the author's point of view, a teacher may meet with small groups and, through a guided discussion, note ideas related to understanding the concept. In both of these cases, teachers should keep observational records that capture evidence of student understanding at a range of levels from concrete to more abstract.

If a paper-and-pencil preassessment is chosen, then it is important to think through how to develop assessment tools to best capture the understanding of the skill, concept, and content. When appropriate, be sure to include both words and pictures in directions and read the directions out loud. Students should also be provided with opportunities to communicate their understanding in various ways. Don't squeeze too many skills or concepts into one preassessment. For example, each math topic or unit can have its own preassessment; it is not appropriate to preassess for an entire year or semester. Besides, how would you preview all of those concepts and skills?

Ideally, preassessments should be built into the curriculum so that teachers do not have to develop them with each new topic or unit and so they can be consistent across classrooms and schools. Regardless of who is creating the assessment, the following should be considered during the development of preassessments:

- The preassessment must measure understanding only in the areas that are specifically being assessed. In other words, if a child's understanding of U.S. history or a student's knowledge of Shakespeare is being assessed, spelling, grammar, and punctuation should not "count." Spelling, grammar, and punctuation have nothing to do with a student's understanding of history or a student's knowledge of Shakespeare. Only if you were specifically assessing spelling, grammar, or punctuation would you consider those errors.
- A preassessment should include application of the skill, topic, or concept and at least one above-level, or accelerated,

standard. You may be surprised at how deep and how far the understanding is for some students.

- When configuring a preassessment, use different formats, allowing students to demonstrate understanding from recognizing an example to producing an example. Formats should vary within the same assessment: creating examples, filling in the blank, open-ended questions, completing a graphic organizer, and/or mind mapping, to name a few. Avoid true/false and other formats where a 50–50 guess exists; for math concepts, assess the concept in two ways if possible.

- Use effective questions. "What kind of candy bar is in the sky?" is an example of a question that was found on a preassessment that was developed to measure student understanding of outer space and the solar system. (The teacher was going for "Milky Way," but "Mars" would also work.) The issue with this question is that it does not give the teacher information. I might know that the Milky Way is in the sky but have no knowledge of what it is. A better way to measure understanding might be the following: "The Milky Way is a galaxy that contains our solar system. Share everything that you know about the Milky Way."

- If reading is not being assessed, read the preassessment to the students. Reading the preassessment levels the playing field for those students who are not yet strong readers. They will be able to demonstrate understanding of the content without worrying about misinterpreting directions or not knowing a word or phrase.

Guidelines for developing a preassessment specific to math can be found in Figure 3.1. Even though these guidelines are directed toward math preassessments, they can be applied to other subject areas as well. Teachers should avoid preassessing and teaching the same topics, skills, procedures, or concepts on the same day. Educators need time to analyze the results and plan for instruction. It is also important to note that preassessments should never count

---

Guidelines for Developing Preassessments for Math

1. The preassessment must measure understanding only in the topic/unit that is specifically being assessed and include both computation/procedural skills and a measurement of conceptual understanding.
2. Make it clear in the teacher resources that teachers should read the preassessment directions out loud so all students understand what is being asked. (A struggling reader should not be penalized in math because he or she cannot read the directions.)
3. Include a few sentences for teachers to read to students prior to the preassessment. This should help frame the reason for the preassessment (i.e., "Today I want to see what you know about fractions. This task will not count as a grade, but it is very important for you to do your best. This will help me plan instruction that is just right for you.").
4. Go deep. A math preassessment is not just about computation. A preassessment should include application of the mathematical skill or concept.
5. When possible, a math preassessment should ask students to reason quantitatively with the concept.
6. When developing a preassessment, use different formats, allowing students to demonstrate understanding from solving a problem to developing a problem. Avoid true/false, multiple choice, and other formats where a students can guess an answer.
7. Assess each math skill or concept in at least two ways.
8. Include above-grade-level standards within the same topic.

Figure 3.1 Guidelines for developing a math-specific preassessment

---

toward a child's grade and that it is important to frame the purpose of the task with the students. Let students know that the information they share will help determine how to approach instruction for them. It is important that they put forth their best effort but that they realize the grade will not count on their report card. One first-grade teacher reported that some of her students cried when completing a preassessment because she did not frame the task properly; they felt frustrated and worried about their lack of knowledge.

When beginning to evaluate student preassessments, another important consideration is how you analyze the outcome. It is not an all-or-nothing approach, and assigning a random percentage is not responsive to specific student needs. Therefore, saying that all students who get an 85% or greater are ready to move on is not appropriate or responsive to students. That randomly assigned number of 85 tells us nothing about where the specific student's strengths and needs lie. The purpose is to find students who have partial or complete understanding, then figure out where the gaps are and how to plan instructionally for those students. When students show partial understanding, note the areas that need to be addressed. This information will help form flexible groups, and the instructional planning that takes place will consider the needs of the students before instruction even begins. Even better, if preassessments are developed centrally in a school district, an electronic tool could be developed that would capture student performance on a preassessment or allow teachers to input data and make recommendations as to the areas that need to be revisited, where content gaps can be filled in, and most importantly, what instruction can be eliminated—in other words, where to compact the curriculum.

Curriculum Compacting

Curriculum compacting was originally developed by Joseph Renzulli and Linda Smith many years ago. It is interesting that it is a relatively "old" strategy that few teachers know about. When preparing to teach graduate school courses on the topic of differentiation, I always send out an electronic preassessment to try to gauge the understanding of the students prior to the start of the course. The results help me adjust the pacing based on the needs of the class as a whole (not to mention that differentiation is being modeled for these grad students). Without fail, every time I analyze the results, the area that surfaces as the greatest need for my students is curriculum compacting. Most don't even know what it is, and the graduate students who know what it is do not know how to implement it.

Curriculum compacting is an instructional strategy that streamlines grade-level curriculum by eliminating content that students have previously learned. Think about what a trash compactor does: it takes a large amount of trash and compacts it down to a little bit of space. Now think about curriculum (I am by no means referring to curriculum as trash 😊): for some students, that big expanse of curriculum can be taught in less time, and some of this curriculum can even be eliminated. Compacting buys time for students to go deeper and wider into the content and/or accelerate to above-grade-level standards. Does every child in your class need the same amount of time to read and discuss a novel? Understand and apply a mathematical process? Educators must be willing to compact curriculum for those students who are ready to go on. How do we know when they are ready?

Curriculum compacting

an instructional strategy that streamlines grade-level curriculum by eliminating content that students have previously learned

The preassessment plays a major role in determining the need for curriculum compacting. Other behaviors in the classroom also give us clues. For example, if a student shows great interest and motivation in a particular area of study, then we know we can move them into deeper understanding of those concepts. For example, Mr. Smith previewed and preassessed student knowledge of World War II, and several students demonstrated a strong conceptual understanding of this time in history. However, Mr. Smith was not really sure about one student, Patrick. Even though Patrick's preassessment results clearly showed some background knowledge of the topic, it was not enough to decide if Patrick needed compacting. Mr. Smith decided to take a few minutes before class to discuss World War II with this student. After only a few minutes, he clearly saw an enthusiastic interest in the topic from Patrick. The student demonstrated a thirst for knowledge in the subject and asked Mr. Smith great questions. This exchange, in combination with the pre-assessment, gave Mr. Smith the data he needed to determine that Patrick needed to be in the compacting group for this unit of study.

Other behaviors that suggest a need for compacting include students who consistently finish work early and accurately and those who express an interest in pursuing advanced topics. Another clue to the need for compacting can surface in those students who often create their own diversions in class. Many of the students who create these distractions do so because they have time to. In other words, they have finished their work and are filling their time with less productive behaviors.

Flexible Grouping

Preassessment and compacting are necessary components when creating flexible small groups in the classroom. Teachers may find that, after preassessment, no students need compacting, that all of the students show enough understanding that they would benefit from taking less time and eliminating material. Also consider that some students have such a deep understanding of a topic that they have no gaps to fill. They don't need compacting; they simply need to move on. Even though the Common Core Standards often go deeper into learning and have more critical thinking embedded than previous standards, it is still important to consider adding a thin layer of enrichment for students who demonstrate mastery before they are accelerated to above-level content. This enrichment will make sure that students are not prematurely moving on. A thin layer means just that: a small amount of enrichment. Spending too much time revisiting and enriching mastered material in new ways does not provide appropriate challenge and is not respectful of the student's prior knowledge.

Maintaining flexible small groups across content areas is an essential component of a differentiated, growth mindset class culture. Historically, elementary classrooms incorporate flexible groups in reading only. Perhaps movement among these groups is not as fluid as it could be, but most primary classrooms operate several reading groups. Over the last several years, I am happy to report that I have observed small flexible group instruction in math in many schools as well. Once students begin middle and high school, an assumption is made that they are "grouped" already. Perhaps a school offers honors or remedial sections in reading or math. Often an assumption is made that subgrouping within a classroom should not occur because of the availability of leveled classes. The fact is that a large range exists within these classes, and differentiation with flexible grouping should be an important tenet of classes that are already homogeneously grouped. Let's go back to the belief that kids can get smarter. If all students in a classroom are instructed at the same level, what opportunities exist to challenge those students who are ready to embrace a more rigorous learning experience? The bottom line is that if we walk into any classroom, in any content area, at any grade level, evidence of flexible small groups should exist. It may not be an everyday occurrence at the secondary level, but it should be an important component of the class structure and used routinely. Teachers often share reasons why flexible grouping does not occur, and the reason that surfaces most often is management. How can we effectively manage multiple groupings in the classroom?

Management

Clear expectations are the single most important aspect of managing multiple groups in the classroom. What are students supposed to do when they are done with their work? What should they do if they need help and you are working with another group of students? Spending time modeling and communicating expectations for independent work time is time well spent. If, for example, three instructional groups exist in a class, then instructional time should occur with each group during the time block. During a 90-minute reading/language arts block in an elementary classroom, the teacher might spend 25 minutes with each group and allow for time between groups to touch base with students to answer any questions and to make sure everyone is on the right track. At the secondary level, a teacher might use a 45-minute period to meet with two groups for 20 minutes each. So, what should students be working on while the teacher is facilitating another group? The other groups should be working on meaningful tasks that will complement the content area they are working on. This might be independent study or could also be a group task.

Carol Ann Tomlinson, who has authored many books on differentiation, suggested incorporating anchor activities into classrooms in her book, *How to Differentiate Instruction in Academically Diverse Classrooms*. Anchor activities are ongoing tasks that students work on independently when they complete classroom work or when their teacher is working with other students. Anchors should enrich the learning of the content being studied. They are similar to centers but are typically available for the duration of a unit of study, quarter, or semester. For example, if students were learning about the election process in the United States, the anchor activities would also be about the election process. Or if you were implementing the professional learning plan for teachers on mindsets and intelligence discussed in Chapter 1, you might provide the following anchor activity to the teachers/staff members:

> If you finish an activity or reading early, please look through this folder and choose an article of interest that discusses various aspects of persistence, motivation, effort, and malleable intelligence.

Anchors can also serve as an opportunity to enrich learning by going deeper into the subject area. These tasks extend the learning and are developed as tasks that can be completed successfully independent of the teacher. Anchor activities are not busy work. They are meaningful tasks that are a natural extension of student learning. Take, for example, a class studying the U.S. election process; the teacher might be extending the learning of a group of students who demonstrated understanding based on a preassessment. The rest of the class is reading and responding to or discussing questions about what they read. Two of these students finish their work so they now have an opportunity to visit some anchor activities. In this case, the teacher has developed an anchor requiring the analysis of political cartoons. The students will access a file of political cartoons from U.S. history that communicate a message about political parties or a special historical election. Using guiding questions and/or a graphic organizer, students analyze the message of the cartoon. They may even categorize cartoons together that send a similar message. This task is meaningful and requires critical thinking while freeing the teacher up to work with another group of students. An added bonus is that this type of anchor does not require a grade, because it is interpretive. The students simply need to put forth effort and justify their thinking.

Anchor activities

ongoing tasks given to students that they can access when they complete classroom work or when their teacher is working with other students, and that enrich the learning of the content being studied

Many resources are available online for developing anchor activities; you may even want to develop some anchors that have to do with the malleability of the brain or neural pathways! It is well worth the time investment, as it will contribute to the successful management of differentiated small-group instruction.

Acceleration and Enrichment

Which is more important: acceleration or enrichment? OK, trick question—they are equally important. Think about enrichment as going deep and wide into the content and acceleration as going forward. Acceleration can take many forms and is not just about grade skipping. It is about allowing students who have already mastered content as evidenced by a preassessment (coupled with observation of students who master content quickly) to move on. Every student deserves to learn every day. Preassessment and curriculum compacting allow for topic/content area acceleration. A growth mindset on the part of both the teacher and the student is necessary for acceleration. We might think things like, "He would not be able to handle acceleration; I don't want to frustrate him," "She gets off task easily, so I will not accelerate," or "They are on a behavior contract." These attempts to rationalize gatekeeping are not part of a responsive classroom. Topic or content area acceleration is not a reward; it is a necessity for those students who have demonstrated mastery and are ready to embrace more challenge.

Acceleration

moving faster through content, allowing students who have already mastered content or who master content quickly to move into above-grade-level content

Enrichment is about going deeper into the learning. Can students apply the skill, concept, or process to different situations? Can they think critically about the content? Do students have the ability to reason with the material? As mentioned above, it is usually a good idea to add at least a thin layer of enrichment before acceleration, especially if the preassessment captures only a surface level of understanding. If the preassessment measures depth of understanding—for example, application of the concept or skill—then perhaps the student is ready to be accelerated without making an enrichment stop. Whether acceleration and/or enrichment occur, it is important to look carefully at instructional experiences to make sure they are laden with opportunities to think critically.

Enrichment

learning with greater depth and breadth;
going deep and wide into the content

Formative Assessment

Formative assessment, or checking for understanding, is non-negotiable in a responsive, growth-mindset classroom. Checking for understanding during the course of instruction contributes to opportunities for students to have access to complex and engaging instruction. It is through formative assessment that educators determine the content and the pace at which students grasp concepts. Through formative assessment, teachers also learn who has not yet grasped a concept and make plans to approach the instruction again in a new way. Ongoing, formative assessment plays a crucial role in teacher decision-making and should be routinely used across all content areas.

Formative assessment

Checking for understanding during the learning process in order to modify instruction to improve understanding; this is an assessment *for* learning

Formative assessment is a reflective tool for a teacher. It should not be graded. It is a quick check to help the teacher become informed of where students are on the path to understanding. Formative assessments help teachers find out who needs to be retaught, who is on track, and who needs enrichment and/or acceleration. If the majority of students do not have success, then teachers should do as Fisher and Frey (2007) noted: reflect on the way the material was taught, come up with a new way to present the material, and reteach it.

Formative assessment is also a checkpoint for student understanding. Teachers can use the data from formative assessments to keep groups fluid and flexible. If a child starts out in an on-level group and comprehends the material at a faster pace than their peer group, then the teacher could move the child to a group that will challenge them. Through ongoing assessment, students will be provided with more opportunities to access enriched learning opportunities.

Formative assessment does not have to be complicated. Keep it simple. The following are a few ideas for implementing formative assessment in your classroom:

- *Use questions for students to respond to orally.* During the course of instruction or on the way out of the door (in middle school and high school), ask students to respond to various questions regarding the learning that occurred during class. Make note of those students who have misunderstandings or have not yet grasped the learning. (This method can also help some students focus their attention during the learning if they know they will be asked about it during or after class.)
- *Use questions for students to respond to in writing.* Provide students with a few questions that will help them communicate their understanding of a concept.
- *Use exit cards.* Provide a prompt on an exit card that each student fills out at the end of an instructional experience. It might be a math problem, a sentence that needs grammar corrections, a question about why or how an historical event came to be, or a statement asking for a summary of the content learned.
- *Use a 3–2–1.* A 3–2–1 can be customized depending on the content and grade level. A generic form of a 3–2–1 might provide students an opportunity to express orally or in writing

---

Formative Assessment About the Brain

Name _____ Date _____

3	Things I learned:
2	Things I have a question about:
1	Thing about the brain that I want to learn more about:

Figure 3.2 Example of a 3-2-1 formative assessment

---

the following: 3 Things I Learned Today, 2 Things I Have Questions About, 1 Thing That I Want to Learn More About. See Figure 3.2 for an example of a 3–2–1.

- *Listen to and observe students.* Observing students during a science lab, working a math problem, or completing an in-class writing assignment, or listening to them discussing a novel, can also serve as a formative assessment.
- *Use a Frayer Model.* Ask students to provide examples, non-examples, list characteristics, and create a visual representation of a concept (see Figure 3.3).

The Association for Middle Level Education offers *8 Digital Formative Assessment Tools to Improve Motivation* which can be found here: https://www .amle.org/8-digital-formative-assessment-tools-to -improve-motivation/

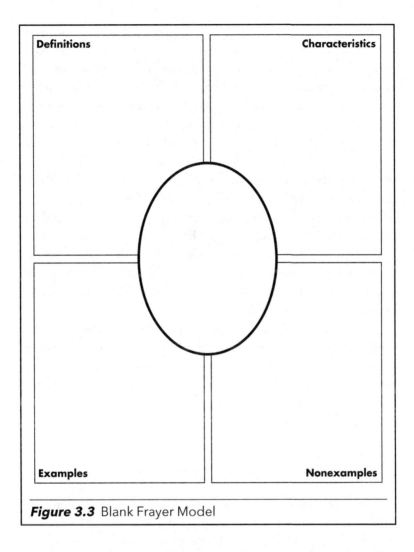

Figure 3.3 Blank Frayer Model

Without formative assessment, the following scenario is bound to happen frequently: a science teacher introduces a new concept to a class of students. He lectures for about 40 minutes using a PowerPoint presentation and explaining the concept. For homework, each student is given a worksheet to complete based on the information he taught that day. Students do the homework and turn it in. After checking their grades online, many find that they received an "F" for their homework.

Now, let's think about this for a minute. The homework could have served as a formative assessment had the teacher approached it differently. After glancing at the homework at the beginning of class, he could have seen that many of the students did not have an understanding of the concept. At that point, he could have used time to go over the homework, clarify, and reteach if necessary. If anchor activities were in place in the class, then the few students who showed mastery might be given the choice to do them or to participate in the clarification/reteaching session. Another concern is that the students did not get the papers back to see where the errors were; they simply saw a grade online. The teacher was holding off giving back the papers until an absent student had the chance to turn his in. Homework can be used as a formative assessment (as long as you are sure it is the student's work) and should never receive a letter grade. Grades for homework should indicate completion, not accuracy, especially when students are still on the pathway to understanding.

When implementing formative assessment, let students know why you assess formatively and that it helps you as a teacher adjust and better meet their needs. Let them know that you always want to improve and grow as a teacher. This models a teacher's own growth mindset for his or her students. Formative assessment improves teaching and learning, and it allows for growth in all students.

Summative Assessment

You have previewed, preassessed, compacted the curriculum for some learners, formed instructional groups, and provided opportunities for enriched learning and accelerated content. Whew! Well done. Now it is time to think about how you will assess understanding or mastery of the content. Giving the same summative assessment (assessment *of* the learning), performance task, or product assignment is not an option when working with different instructional groups. The assessment must match the learning that has taken place for each group or, in some cases, an individual student. If students will be demonstrating understanding through a product, then make sure choices are offered. Grades (ugh!) should be based on mastery of the content that was tailored to the student. If grades were given solely on mastery of on-grade-level curriculum, then students could potentially earn an A after the preassessment, before any instruction even occurred. In this scenario, a child has put forth no effort and yet is "rewarded" with an A. It is this kind of situation that contributes to the development of a fixed mindset. Students begin to feel that they must always look smart, that putting forth effort shows weakness, and that they are expected to know things without trying. After all, their whole lives they have been told they are "smart," and if you are smart, everything should come easy, right? Wrong. Students must be challenged appropriately. Be sure that your assessments, both formative and summative, are differentiated for each group.

Summative assessment

assessment *of* learning that typically occurs at the end of a unit of study

TEACHER MINDSETS MATTER

A study conducted by Miele, Perez, and Butler looked at the relationship between teachers' mindsets and the instructional practices that they use individually with students on both ends of the achievement spectrum.

The researchers hypothesized that fixed mindset teachers would likely engage in instructional practices that were more "controlling" or teacher-led when working with students with a perceived lower ability level. The study concluded that teachers with what they describe as a "weaker growth mindset" may believe that low-ability students cannot succeed on their own, so therefore they need to have more controlling instructional practices. Implications from the study suggest that "encouraging teachers to adopt growth mindsets may help them develop instructional practices that are equally constructive for all students."

A Final Thought About Differentiated, Responsive Instruction

What I refer to as front-end differentiated, responsive instruction is about respecting and responding to what a child needs when they walk in the door and as they make their way through the learning. Too often, differentiation occurs on the back end of instruction. The teacher figures out at the end of a unit or learning sequence that a student needs more. The "more" is too often interpreted as more of the same or more papers or "activities" rather than more teacher-directed responsive instruction. Provide opportunities for students to be challenged from the beginning. Be responsive to their needs and the potential of all they can accomplish.

Template for Planning

In Figures 3.4 and 3.5, you will find a template that helps visualize the differentiation/responsive teaching process and a checklist for you to use as you begin the process.

The template in Figure 3.4 is a way to reflect on, think about, and set up the instruction; it does not include specific instructional strategies. However, care should be taken to differentiate processes or strategies among the groups. Differentiation of process is about how the learning is presented and how a student interacts with the material. Also note that the differentiation model described is focused on readiness, not student interest; student interest should be considered when planning an instructional sequence. Many teachers find this template helpful for planning for differentiation. Once educators internalize the process, this planning shell may not be needed. Several teachers use the template to record the names of the students in each group on the back of each column or replicate the template electronically and record student data; this can serve as a way to keep track of where students begin and how far they go in a specific unit, topic, or concept.

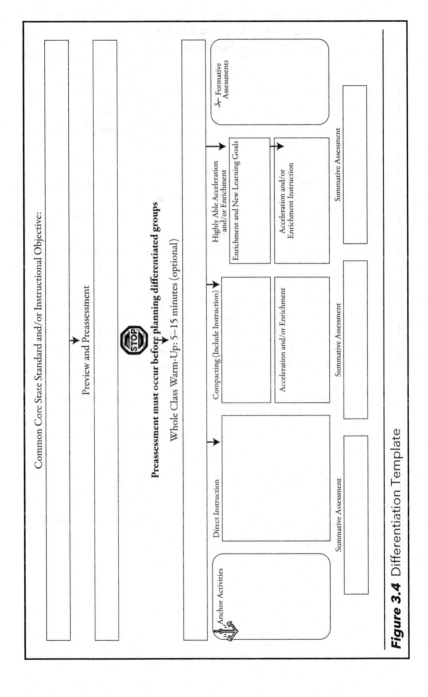

Figure 3.4 Differentiation Template

Teacher Checklist for Planning
Differentiated, Responsive Instruction

☐ Determine standards, skills, content, concepts, or procedures being assessed and develop or use school/district preassessment.

☐ Develop or find web based anchor activities related to the unit.

☐ Present preview (2–5 minutes) to activate background knowledge prior to preassessment.

☐ Students take preassessment.

☐ Analyze preassessments: Determine areas already mastered, any gaps that may exist, and areas of need for each student.

☐ Identify students who would benefit from curriculum compacting and plan instruction for the areas of need.

☐ Identify any students who have complete understanding and are ready for a new learning outcome. Plan for enrichment and topic/content acceleration for these students.

☐ Form instructional groups—model anchor activity expectations if necessary and share the group rotation for the day. Teacher will instruct each group every day. Plan for a few minutes between groups to respond to any questions from students, make sure everyone is on the right track, and praise effort students are putting forth.

☐ Administer formative assessment daily. Use the information to inform instruction for students as well as reflection for the teacher. If understanding is not evident with most students, reteach in a new way. Student movement among groups may occur based on the formative assessments.

☐ Summative assessments, performance tasks, and products (as well as homework) should be differentiated based on the instruction for each group.

Figure 3.5 Differentiation Checklist

With practice, effort, motivation, and, yes, a growth mindset, differentiated, responsive instruction can become the heart of instruction. Responding to the needs of all learners is a responsibility that we all have as educators.

References

Fisher, D., & Frey, N. (2007). *Checking for understanding: Formative assessment techniques for your classroom.* Alexandria, VA: Association for Supervision and Curriculum Development.

Miele, D. B., Perez, S. A., & Butler, R. (2017). Elementary school teachers' academic mindsets predict their differential treatment of low and high ability students. Paper presented at the annual meeting of the American Educational Research Association, San Antonio, TX.

Renzulli, J. S., & Smith, L. H. (1979). *A guidebook for developing individualized educational programs for gifted and talented students.* Mansfield Center, CT: Creative Learning Press.

Sousa, D. A., & Tomlinson, C. A. (2011). *Differentiation and the brain: How neuroscience supports the learner-friendly classroom.* Bloomington, IN: Solution Tree Press.

Tomlinson, C. A. (2017). *How to differentiate instruction in academically diverse classrooms*, 3rd ed. Alexandria, VA: Association for Supervision and Curriculum Development.

CHAPTER 4

WHY IS CRITICAL THINKING IMPORTANT IN A GROWTH MINDSET CLASS CULTURE?

"I don't mind if I mess up an assignment, as long as I figure out what I did wrong."
–Grade 6 student

What is the relationship between critical thinking and growth mindset? Let's first take a moment and agree on a definition of critical thinking. Daniel Willingham, professor of cognitive psychology at the University of Virginia, gave solid research on the development of critical thinking in our schools. Willingham shared that, from a cognitive scientist's point of view, three types of thinking fall under the umbrella of critical thinking: reasoning, making judgments/decisions, and problem-solving. Every day we reason, problem solve, and make decisions, but they do not always require critical thought. For example, when you woke up this morning one of the first decisions that you had to make was what to wear. Is this a decision that required critical thought? In most cases, no; however, is there ever a time when deciding what to wear does require critical thought? Perhaps if you were planning a day of hiking in a terrain where temperatures can change dramatically or you had an important job interview; in these cases, deciding what to wear could require a small degree of critical thought. Students may be given opportunities to reason, make decisions, or problem solve, but the question we must ask ourselves as educators is if these opportunities require deep, critical thinking.

Another important factor to consider about critical thinking is that it is not a simple skill. According to Willingham (2008), critical thinking is a process that must be infused with content; it is not something that you can just check off a list once it is mastered. Why? Well, one reason is that the content being focused on and the complexity of thinking critically become more sophisticated as students grow intellectually—it is always evolving. The practice component applied to the content knowledge is essential to develop learners who can apply critical thinking when they need to. Hand in hand with practice is perseverance and resiliency—probably the two most important attributes of having a growth mindset!

If you embrace Willingham's argument that critical thinking is not a bunch of isolated skills, then you too (like me) may become bothered by the amount of resources on the market that advertise ways to build critical thinking "skills." Due in part to the way critical thinking is framed in these resources, the concept of accepting critical thinking as a process embedded in content rather than a set of skills can require a major shift in thinking.

Critical Thinking in School

During a professional learning workshop, one teacher disagreed with the notion that critical thinking is not a skill. In the process of her disagreement, she explained that cooking is a skill that can never be mastered because the complexity grows, just like thinking critically. I knew where she was coming from—she made the assumption that cooking itself was a skill. Not so—it is a process that requires many skills. She was correct in her analogy that cooking can become more complex just like critical thinking, and she provided me with an opportunity to expand her analogy. Cooking is not a skill but a process, a process that requires certain skills: measurement skills, knife skills, following directions, reading skills, etc. Critical thinking is a process that also requires skills. The skills required vary depending on the situation. For example, if a student is required to analyze data, he may need to use classification skills. The skill of classifying can be taught, practiced, and applied to a variety of situations from an early age. We want to start thinking about critical thinking as a process of strategies that can be applied to myriad situations rather than a set of skills.

Often, expectations are low for students who do not show strength in the traditional areas of schooling: reading, writing, and math. When students are viewed through a lens of achievement (or intelligence in some cases), opportunities for critical thinking are fewer for those students who are on the perceived lower end. Unfortunately, it usually boils down to what reading or math level they are functioning on. Students who are from culturally, linguistically, and/or ethnically diverse populations, special education students, and yes, even sometimes those students who demonstrate challenging behaviors, are often not provided with rigorous instructional opportunities. These students would benefit tremendously from ongoing, critical thinking experiences, yet these are the students who typically get the fewest critical thinking opportunities thanks to a fixed mindset from the point of view of adults or the students themselves. By providing students with many opportunities to develop their cognitive abilities through critical thinking experiences, it impacts the child's view of themselves and contributes to a growth mindset.

The Critical Thinking Growth Mindset Project

I was anxious to test my theory about how cognitive abilities can be changed through critical thinking experiences in schools with high poverty and lower achievement and developed a program that would put it to the test. Hence, the *Critical Thinking Growth Mindset Project* was born. This project involved six Title I (high poverty) schools, with a total of 53 grade 2 and grade 3 classrooms. All grade 2 and grade 3 teachers, as well as some English Language Learner (ELL) teachers, in these Title I schools attended ongoing professional learning sessions that focused on building a growth mindset culture in their classrooms. The professional development also included critical thinking professional learning sessions. Part of the critical thinking professional learning sessions highlighted places where critical thinking processes were already embedded in their curriculum. Consideration of the critical thinking that is embedded in the Common Core State Standards for Mathematical Practice was also highlighted. Several of these eight mathematical practices complemented the goals of the project, with practices #1 and #2 being the most emphasized.

- CCSS Mathematical Practice #1: make sense of problems and persevere in solving them.
- CCSS Mathematical Practice #2: reason abstractly and quantitatively.
- CCSS Mathematical Practice #3: construct viable arguments and critique the reasoning of others.
- CCSS Mathematical Practice #5: use appropriate tools strategically.

Professional learning workshops during the first year of the project focused on ways that teachers could build students' reasoning abilities; therefore, the teachers learned instructional strategies that develop reasoning across all content areas. These included strategies that focused on deductive, analogical, and quantitative reasoning, as well as concept attainment and concept formation strategies. (Note that several of these strategies are embedded in the student lessons that were provided for the teachers.)

Nonverbal Reasoning Games

Embedding opportunities to reason in different ways with a variety of materials as often as possible was a goal for these classrooms. It was decided that another layer would be added by introducing some engaging nonverbal reasoning games into the classrooms. But first, it was important to allow teachers to interact with these games so that they could really understand the challenge that students would face while progressing through the levels of the games. After review of many games, it was decided that each of the 53 classrooms would receive five specially selected games from ThinkFun, a company that specializes in developing games that build reasoning skills. The games that were chosen—ShapeOmetry, Chocolate Fix, Brick by Brick, Rush Hour, and Math Dice Jr.— specifically practiced quantitative and deductive reasoning in a non-verbal format. The games also increased the level of challenge as the children made their way up through each level. The project now had three important components:

1. Teachers and students building a growth mindset culture, including development of a conceptual understanding of basic brain function.
2. Teachers using instructional strategies that nurtured and developed critical thinking processes, specifically reasoning.
3. Access to nonverbal reasoning games that would be used as math anchor activities or warm-ups and would be available during inside recess, before and after school, etc.

All teachers were asked to record any instruction that focused on building a growth mindset culture, teaching students about the brain, and critical thinking using an electronic implementation tracker. Students were responsible for keeping track of the games they played and the levels they reached using an individual game tracker.

As a result of adding the specifically chosen reasoning games to the project, an outcome surfaced that was unexpected. The addition of the games did something more than build the reasoning abilities of these students; the reasoning and problem-solving games contributed to a mindset shift in the teachers and, in some cases, the students as well. Many teachers reported that they saw potential in students that they would have never seen without the games. Some of the students who spoke little English flourished when the games came out. Some students who were functioning below grade level showed great strength in reasoning through playing these games. Teachers became more reflective about their own mindsets, viewed students differently, and raised expectations for many students. The games became an unexpected vehicle for building growth mindsets in the teachers and the students. As Holly, one of the third-grade ELL teachers, reported:

> I first taught the game to my struggling ELL students, giving them plenty of time to become familiar with the game and to formulate strategies for problem-solving. Once they were comfortable and conversant about their strategies, I sent them out into the classroom to "teach" the rest of the class how to play. This was a powerful tool for their language development, as well as their self-esteem. These games contributed greatly to the growth mindset culture being developed in the class.

The games, in partnership with growth mindset lessons, also appeared to increase motivation for students. About four weeks into the project, I was visiting a classroom to demonstrate how neurons connected every time the students learned something new. After the lesson, the teacher was going right into math instructional time and had partnered students together to work with games that specifically focused on quantitative reasoning (ShapeOmetry) while she worked with a small group of students at her table. I decided to walk around this second-grade classroom and ask the students some questions as they played their reasoning games. With their permission, I used my phone to record these conversations. Here is an example of one of those conversations with two ELL boys as they played ThinkFun's ShapeOmetry:

Mrs. Ricci: So what's going on in your brain when you are playing this game?
Students: We are making connections.
Mrs. Ricci: What kinds of connections?
Students: Connections like those…what are the names of those? Numerals?
Mrs. Ricci: Neurons?
Students: Yes, those neurons are sticking together in my head.
Mrs. Ricci: Do you ever feel like giving up?
Students: No, never.
Mrs. Ricci: Why?
Students: It is easy.
Mrs. Ricci: Was it always easy?
Students: No, not always easy.
Mrs. Ricci: Why is it easier now?
Students: We just, well we did it for about five days, and it got easier because we practiced.
Mrs. Ricci: Oh, so you practiced? So the more you practiced, then what happened?
Students: We made more connections in our brains, and it gets easier!

You can see from that short conversation that these students are visualizing neural connections as they learn. Even though the child said "numerals" instead of "neurons" and said they were "sticking together in my head" rather than "making connections in my brain," he still had a solid conceptual understanding of what was happening, and that understanding increased his perseverance and motivation to get through the tougher levels of the game. This can then be transferred to situations where a child might be struggling. For example, a teacher might say:

Do you remember when you first played ShapeOmetry and it was hard? You practiced and persevered and made strong connections in your brain. Is it still just as hard for you? Now let's look at math the same way. It might feel very challenging at first, but with practice and perseverance you are making more connections in your brain and soon it will be easy!

Referring back to the process the students went through using the reasoning game helped get the conversation going about staying motivated when faced with challenging tasks. In some cases, students asked for "harder stuff" to help their brains grow.

The following is another example of a dialogue with two ELL grade 2 students playing Rush Hour. The students began by explaining to me how to play the game. Then the conversation continued with one of the students:

> *Mrs. Ricci:* Do you ever feel like giving up?
> *Student:* No!
> *Mrs. Ricci:* Why?
> *Student:* I would give up playing a game like…
> Hide and Go Seek, but not this game.
> *Mrs. Ricci:* Why wouldn't you give up playing this game?
> *Student:* I am not giving up!
> *Mrs. Ricci:* Tell me why.
> *Student:* Well, first I think it is above grade level, and I think I can really do this thing!
> *Mrs. Ricci:* What makes you think that you can do it?
> *Student:* Because when I try, I know I am getting smarter by making connections, and the new connections will help me do it!

This dialogue is such a wonderful example of student perseverance. The reference he made to "above grade level" made it clear that in his mind he was tackling a very challenging task. What a great example of a student welcoming challenge! He was determined to have success. His reference to Hide and Go Seek was interesting. Perhaps he does not view Hide and Go Seek as strategic or challenging; therefore, he would give up because it would not be giving his brain a workout. In all eight informal interviews that were conducted with these groups of students, not one student said that he or she ever felt like giving up. As one of the ELL students put it, "The more you try, the more you get smarter." Many teachers reported that they felt the games coupled with the growth mindset discussions increased perseverance. I suspect that if the games were just placed in the classrooms without the benefits of the growth mindset lessons and discussions, these conversations would have played out differently. My hunch is that many of these students would have given up at an early level of the game.

Results of the Critical Thinking Growth Mindset Project

The Critical Thinking Growth Mindset Project showed unexpected results in just seven months. Not only did the teachers report increased motivation and persistence, but also the data showed growth in reasoning for the students in these schools. Part of the school district's process for "Gifted and Talented" screening was the use of a cognitive abilities test. Scores from Title I schools were consistently well below the target score. In order to be considered for accelerated and/or enriched instruction, as well as identified as "Gifted," this system used multiple criteria, rather than relying solely on a test score. One criterion was a target score of the 80th percentile on analogical and quantitative reasoning subtests of a cognitive abilities test. In the spring of their second-grade year, students across the district participated in a process for gifted services and identification. The mean scores for the six schools are shown in Table 4.1.

You can see how depressed these scores were. After just seven months into the project, scores improved dramatically (see Table 4.2).

Table 4.1
Mean Scores for Students Before the Critical Thinking Growth Mindset Project

	Analogical Reasoning Percentile Mean Score	Quantitative Reasoning Percentile Mean Score	Target Percentile
2011	51	43	80
2010	50	43	80

Table 4.2
Scores of Students After Seven Months in the Critical Thinking Growth Mindset Project

	Analogical Reasoning Percentile Mean Score	Quantitative Reasoning Percentile Mean Score	Target Percentile
2012	59 (+8)	50 (+7)	80
2011	51	43	80
2010	50	43	80

All six schools averaged growth of 8 percentile points in analogical reasoning and 7 percentile points in quantitative reasoning.

One school made a jump of 21 percentile points on the quantitative reasoning subtest, and another jumped 14 points in analogical reasoning. Although there is still a long way to go to get close to the benchmark, we realized that we were onto something. That "something" is the combination of a growth mindset partnered with increased opportunities for critical thinking. Take a look at the following comments made by some of the teachers at the end of the first year of the project:

- "The perspective of students shifted completely. Whenever there was a difficult task, students would talk about determination, motivation, and persistence."

- "I found that their beliefs about how they can 'grow smart' changed as they would encourage each other by saying things like, 'You can do it!' and 'You can get smarter if you try harder!'"
- "My students constantly referred to having a growth mindsets when setbacks occurred; it was great!"
- "I noticed a huge difference in student critical thinking as well as students' core beliefs that they could try hard and keep trying and succeed. I heard much less 'I can't' and more 'I have to keep trying.'"
- "Thinking and working hard became a 'mindset' in my classroom. We all worked together, learned from our mistakes, and challenged our brains to grow. The students have become really good at believing in themselves."

Critical thinking and a growth mindset culture go hand in hand. We can expect students to embrace challenge only if we make it available to them on a consistent basis.

References

Willingham, D. T. (2008). Critical thinking: Why is it so hard to teach? *Arts Education Policy Review, 109*(4), 21–32. https://doi .org/10.3200/AEPR.109.4.21-32.

CHAPTER 5

HOW CAN STUDENTS LEARN FROM FAILURE?

"Failure is necessary for success. The more we try to avoid it, the less successful we are. Failure should be embraced, not avoided."–Grade 12 student

Perhaps a better title for this chapter would be "Why do we need to deliberately cultivate perseverance and resiliency in our students?" The development of these noncognitive skills is instrumental when working toward framing mistakes and failure as a learning experience.

Over the years, I have determined that perhaps the most important of these is resiliency. We know that some of our students may demonstrate resiliency outside of school—perhaps they go home to a stressful household or live in a neighborhood that requires resilient behaviors. Many of our students have also had traumatic events in their lives. The National Child Traumatic Stress Network (NCTSN) resource, *Resilience and Child Traumatic Stress*, provides adults with a background about childhood trauma.

DOI: 10.4324/9781003406914-5

One of the most helpful sections of this resource is a list of factors that can lead to enhanced resilience in children after traumatic events. Here are a few of those factors:

- Support from parents, friends, family, school, and community.
- Resources that help to buffer negative consequences on daily life.
- Feeling safe at home, school, and in the community.
- Having high self-esteem—an overall positive sense of self-worth.
- Possessing a sense of self-efficacy—a child's belief that he or she can be successful in different areas of life (growth mindset!!).
- Having a sense of meaning in one's life, which might include spiritual or cultural beliefs, connections with others, or goals and dreams.
- Possessing a variety of adaptive and flexible coping skills that he or she can use in different situations.

It is important to remember that some of our students have life circumstances that can hinder the development of resilience. Violence in their neighborhood, illness, racism, and poverty are just a few things that can undermine becoming resilient individuals.

The kind of resiliency that may be demonstrated outside of school does not easily translate into the kind of resiliency needed in school. Academic resiliency is what we strive for—that ability to bounce back from setbacks that may occur in the learning process. What is a typical response or behavior from a student who has "hit the wall," is frustrated, or doesn't understand? It is likely that they will give up. Students may say things like "This is too hard," "I can't understand this," or "This is dumb." Students need to learn that struggle is a very important part of the learning process. Embrace the struggle.

Academic resiliency cannot be developed if students are under-challenged. If there has never been a "struggle" or a failure, there has never been an opportunity to bounce back from anything.

> *Academic resiliency cannot be developed if students are underchallenged.*

As a parent, it is always difficult to see one of my children fail, especially if much effort was put into undertaking the task. Think about the child who dedicates themselves to studying for a test, working on a paper, or practicing a skill, and then the reward is failure. Reward? Yes, failure can be a reward, for it is through failure that we can learn the most. There is a wonderful scene in Disney's *Meet the Robinsons* movie where Lewis creates an invention that combines peanut butter and jelly and it fails. As he buries his face in his hands and apologizes, the adults happily yell, "You've failed! From failure, you learn. From success…not so much."

That brings me to a study, *Learning from your Mistakes: Does It Matter If You're Out in Left Foot, I Mean Field?* (Cyr & Anderson, 2018) No, not a typo, I love the name of this article that describes the outcome of this study because it kind of says it all. The researchers found that mistakes that are almost correct can help learners acquire information better than if no error occurred at all. Why? Because the almost correct answer becomes a clue for remembering the information in the future.

Responding to Failure

The way we respond to failures and mistakes depends on our mindset. When we truly believe that intelligence is malleable, it is then that we realize that when we make a mistake—when we fail—we need to approach the task differently and/or put more effort into it. On the other hand, those who hold a fixed view of intelligence typically do not attempt to learn from their errors. Jason S. Moser of Michigan State University (who collaborated on his study with Hans S. Schroder, Carrie Heeter, Tim P. Moran, and Yu-Hao Lee) wanted some insight as to how people react to failure. These researchers gave participants a task that was purposefully designed for them to experience an error. Study subjects were asked to name the middle letter of a five-letter series. Sometimes the middle letter was the same as all of the other letters, like MMMMM; other times the middle letter was different, like MMNMM. Even though the task sounds simple, once this is repeated several times, the brain can get sluggish, which is when people can begin to make mistakes.

Participants in the study wore a contraption on their head that recorded brain activity. Once a mistake occurred, within a quarter of a second, the brain made two quick symbols. First, an initial response that something was not right, an "oh crap response," according to Moser and his colleagues. The next signal occurred when the person realized the error and subsequently attempted to correct it. What the study found is that those who produced a bigger second signal—the signal that caused people to recognize the error then try to correct it—were the people who tended to learn from their mistakes. These were the people who could better redirect their thinking to saying, "OK, that wasn't right; now let's see what I need to do to correct it." This group of people took the opportunity to learn from their errors.

When students consciously take the opportunity to learn from all of their errors, they will approach the unsuccessful task in a new way or with more effort. Students who believe that the negative outcome is based on their natural ability will often not bother to try harder after failure; it is then that we hear phrases like, "I am just not good at science," "I will never be able to learn another language," or "It doesn't matter if I do it again; I will have the same results."

Angel Pérez, former dean of admission at Pitzer College in California, interviewed many students who applied for admission to his institution and always asked potential students the same question, "What do you look forward to the most in college?" On one occasion, he heard a response that took him by surprise: "I look forward to the possibility of failure." This potential student continued, "You see, my parents have never let me fail…taking a more rigorous course or trying an activity I may not succeed in, they tell me, will ruin my chances at college admission" (Pérez, 2012, para. 2).

Learning to embrace failure is hardly easy; however, once again, if students learn more about their brains and how it works, failure becomes easier to handle. Students who internalize the understanding of the plasticity of the brain and the functional changes in the brain that occur when we learn can deal more constructively with setbacks. They are sometimes even more motivated to work toward mastery and will persist and persevere until they do.

Educators who value the importance of providing challenging opportunities for students find that students react to the challenge in different ways. Some students have a "Bring it on!" approach and embrace the challenge with enthusiasm. These students realize that they may not be successful and might even fail at a task or two, but want to take the risk and stretch themselves. Other students feel threatened by the challenge, are afraid they will not succeed, and will often give up before they put much effort into it.

It is imperative that teachers develop a climate in their classroom where failure is viewed as an expected and very important part of the learning process, and students learn to reflect and redirect so that they can approach a challenging task in a new way or with more effort. Teachers can model this behavior themselves in the classroom.

Motivation

It is hard to discuss failure without also considering motivation. Social scientist Bernard Weiner (1974, 1980) is best known for his work with attribution theory. Weiner's theory focuses on motivation and achievement, and he considers the most important factors affecting achievement to be ability, effort, task difficulty, and luck. Any of those factors sound familiar? Weiner's research on effort was the precursor to growth mindset theory. According to the attribution theory, successful people will often attribute their success to effort, an internal factor. Those who are unsuccessful tend to attribute their lack of success or failure to the difficulty of the task and/or to just having bad luck. Our goal is to encourage students to internalize the belief that their own actions and behaviors, not external factors, guide them to achievement.

Attribution theory

a theory that suggests that successful people will often attribute their success to effort (an internal factor) while those who are unsuccessful tend to attribute their lack of success or failure to the difficulty of the task and/or to just having bad luck (external factors)

In Daniel Pink's book, *Drive: The Surprising Truth About What Motivates Us*, he presents a good case for intrinsic rather than extrinsic rewards. Intrinsic rewards refer to the personal satisfaction a person feels when something is accomplished, when no outside incentives are in place. Extrinsic rewards come from an outside place, usually a teacher or a parent who promises a prize, sticker, even money if a child demonstrates success. (Even grades, especially when they are tied to other incentives, serve as extrinsic motivators. We'll talk more about grades in a moment.) Pink shows how this can affect a student's performance when he writes,

> In environments where extrinsic rewards are most salient, many people work only to the point that triggers the reward—and no further. So if students get a prize for reading three books, many won't pick up a fourth, let alone embark on a lifetime of reading. (p. 58)

Pink goes on to explain that the practice of trying to motivate by promising rewards has many flaws. Extinguishing student creativity and fostering short-term thinking are a few issues that can surface when students are promised a "reward" to reach a predetermined goal. Instead, the "reward" can be the praise students receive regarding the effort and persistence they put forth coupled with that positive internal feeling that we all get when we have mastered something new. Accomplishing a challenging task is inherently enjoyable.

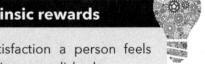

Intrinsic rewards

the personal satisfaction a person feels when something is accomplished.

Extrinsic rewards

outside incentives provided to a person by another individual or source, such as money, certificates, or prizes

Grades

I am just going to put this out there—grades and growth mindset are not a happy union. Why? Because grades emphasize the end result, not the process. The process and the end result (the grade) are not necessarily connected—some students get A's with very little effort while others work hard for B's and C's. (Note that standards-based grading is more growth-mindset friendly—either a child has mastered the standard or is not there "yet.")

Think about some ways that we can use the act of grading a paper to build on the concept of learning from failure. Here is a simple idea: instead of putting an "X" next to an incorrect response (yes, this is still a practice in some classrooms) just circle the response—let students know that whenever they see a circle on their work it means "Look at this again" or "You don't quite get this yet." Then, provide the opportunity for them to reflect, revisit, and/or ask for clarification or reteaching about the item(s). If we really believe in the importance of learning from errors, we should allow students to redo assignments and retake assessments.

The growth mindset educator will work with students and guide or help them to approach the learning in a new way. We also need to provide time and space for practice and feedback. According to education author Rick Wormeli (2011):

> Many teachers reason that they are building moral fiber and preparing students for the working world by denying them the opportunity to redo assignments and assessments—or if they do allow retakes, by giving only partial credit for redone assessments even when students have demonstrated full mastery of the content. These are the same teachers who set a deadline for submitting work and then give students who do not meet the deadline a zero, thinking that the devastating score will teach them responsibility.
>
> In reality, these practices have the opposite effect: They retard student achievement and maturation. As hope wanes, resentment builds. Without hope—especially hope that teachers see the moral, competent, and responsible self inside them, waiting to shed its immature shell—students disengage from the school's mission and the adults who care for them. Our education enterprise is lost. (p. 22–26)

Allowing redo's allows students to learn from their errors and, most importantly, learn and master the material that is being taught.

Another strategy that can be used is one called "My Favorite Mistakes". As you grade an assignment, test, or unit assessment, make note of some errors that you feel would provide an opportunity for students to better understand or internalize a concept. Either before or after passing back the reviewed assessments, let the students know that you had some favorite mistakes that you wanted to share with the class.

You can then use this opportunity to go over them with the entire class or a small group. A video of seventh- and eighth-grade math teacher Leah Alcala implementing this strategy is a must-see. *Highlighting Mistakes—A Grading Strategy* can be found at https://www.youtube.com/watch?v=BO2gndc4d9I. In Leah's class, she does not put a grade on the paper; students can check the grading portal for a grade if they wish. Rather than circling items, she highlights them—her focus is on the process, the learning, the review, not the grade. This contributes to helping students frame mistakes or failures as a learning tool. As you watch, listen carefully as the students process the errors and to how Leah responds.

Changing How Students React to Failure

When students fail or have many errors, they may look at this as a sign of weakness and incompetence within themselves, which can actually lead to more failure. They may begin to avoid anything that looks remotely challenging so that they do not have to face failure. They may become "risk-averse." On the other hand, if students look at failure or errors as a way to get feedback or reflect on areas that need more attention, they possess an underlying belief that they will, with effort, perseverance, and help (ideally, that they've sought out themselves), eventually grasp the learning.

Every time teachers help students with an error, they should seize this opportunity to help students interpret the errors as "data" that will help them later, rather than looking at themselves through a lens of low ability. For example, if a student is struggling with solving a math word problem, a teacher should ask the student what strategies they have used and brainstorm some alternative strategies that can be used. Some argue that children from middle- and upper-class homes do not get enough opportunities to fail thanks to well-meaning, but highly overprotective adults who catch them before they fall. This is a fine line to walk for parents because if they choose not to step in to prevent failure, then kids may not feel supported and valued.

In Paul Tough's book, *How Children Succeed: Grit, Curiosity, and the Hidden Power of Character,* Tough claims that grit and persistence are the biggest indicators of student success. He shares that we should be developing a sense of resiliency in the face of failure among our children. Tough recognizes that failure is an important life lesson. However, when faced with failure, it is imperative that opportunities are built where students can reflect and make adjustments or changes so that they learn from the situation.

Tom Kelley and David Kelley, authors of *Creative Confidence: Unleashing the Creative Potential Within Us All,* recommend that we embrace our failures. We must own it. If we don't reflect on our failures and really figure out what went wrong, we will not know how to improve the outcome the next time. As they share, "Acknowledging mistakes is also important for moving on. In doing so, you not only sidestep the psychological pitfalls of cover-up, rationalization, and guilt: you may also find that you enhance your own brand through your honesty, candor, and humility" (2013, p. 51).

One way teachers can help students reflect on failure is to introduce them to a more positive outlook on failure, perhaps by sharing others' attitudes toward failure. For example, cognitive psychologist Jerome Bruner (1961) hit the nail on the head when he framed failure in this way: "Experience success and failure not as a reward and punishment, but as information" (p. 61). Or, as a more contemporary figure, Michael Jordan, summed up failure in a 1997 Nike commercial: "I've missed more than 9,000 shots in my career. I've lost almost 300 games. Twenty-six times I've been trusted to take the game-winning shot...and missed. I've failed over and over and over again in my life. And that is why I succeed."

What's Grit Got to Do With It?

In an NPR interview, researcher Angela Duckworth (the queen of grit) defined grit as a "combination of passion and perseverance for very long-term goals."

I remember talking with a Supervisor of Middle School English in a large school district. The district had just transitioned to using a new computer-adaptive achievement assessment for reading. Students took this assessment two or three times a year in order to measure growth. Middle school teachers in her district reported that they noticed that as the reading passages got longer, students were disengaging, skimming quickly, or not reading the passage at all before answering the questions. They were not willing to put the time in to reading the entire passage—why? Well, one reason is because perhaps they had not yet developed stamina or grit in relation to reading extended pieces of text. It is also likely that some students were just not interested in the task. Interest and grit go hand in hand. According to Duckworth (2016), "Nobody works doggedly on something they don't find intrinsically interesting" (p. 106). Developing interests in specific topics or activities takes exposure and time—it rarely happens after one encounter. From interests, passion can grow. It is in the "passion" zone that we are likely to see people demonstrate grit on a regular basis over a longer period of time.

Concept Development: Grit

Since previous editions of this book, I have backed off a little about promoting grit with all students. It has been my observation (nothing scientific-based, but through my observations of students and discussions with teachers) that the concept of grit is best introduced after students have internalized the concepts of perseverance and resilience—somewhere around the age of 13. At that time, students can work to conceptualize what grit is and what it is not. So, how do we build the concept of grit?

A group of eighth-grade students were learning about growth mindset with specific focus on the brain, perseverance, and resiliency. Their teacher invited me in to discuss the concept of grit. I rounded up three samples of sandpaper with varying degrees of grit: fine, medium, and coarse. I asked students to study these samples carefully and note the differences. We talked a little about what sandpaper is typically used for, and then I asked them why they thought it came in a range of grittiness. I then asked them if they saw any similarities between the different sandpaper and how they faced a difficult task. Responses included the following:

- The smoother sandpaper is like when you don't have to try too hard—just "lightly" trying.
- The medium sandpaper is when you have to persevere in order to get something accomplished.
- The coarse sandpaper is when you have to get through a lot of rough spots and it takes a lot more effort to understand or to get something done.

I followed up with this question and asked them to discuss it with a partner: "Is there ever a time when you might need to use all three?" After hearing some energetic discussions, several groups shared a scenario similar to the following:

> Sometimes something is so challenging that you spend a long time trying to understand it, and when you think you have it, another obstacle pops up—this is like the coarse sandpaper. You need to get through that tough part first, and it takes a long time. Once you get through that, you can pay more attention to the details—this is where the medium sandpaper comes in. Then finally you get to the point where you need to practice so that you will really remember and understand—this is like the fine sandpaper, paying attention to every little detail.

I explained that the coarse sandpaper was the one with the most "grit" and asked them to surmise what they thought it meant to be "gritty" or have grit.

On my next visit, I gave each student a small stack of sticky notes and asked them to independently write one idea about grit on each note. Some used only one note; others used up to five sticky notes. When they completed this task, they were asked to go up to the board (wall, window, floor, any open space works) and place their idea next to another note that had the same or similar idea. (This was done in silence—no discussion took place.) At the activity's conclusion, the class had categorized similar ideas about grit together. A few outlier responses stood alone. Students then collaborated to come up with category names for each group. For example, "Athletic Grit" included responses like running a marathon, daily weight lifting, and four hours of practice each day. Another category, "School Grit," included things like studying for weeks for a test, pushing through a challenge, and having a growth mindset (I particularly liked this response!). I am not going to share the other categories with you in case you feel the urge to make suggestions to your students—stay out of this process and let the students determine categories. In some cases, they may even have a lively discussion about moving some responses into other categories. It will also be interesting to note how your students respond to the task—some will provide examples like the ones above, and others may just write words like *rough, strong, tough, sticking with something, determination.*

Other discussions that will contribute to building the concept of grit could be focused around the following:

- Share some examples of a time when you demonstrated grit.
- Think of some people who have demonstrated grit in their lifetimes.
- Can anything other than people demonstrate grit? (Animals? Machines?)
- Think of a time when you did not demonstrate grit and you wished you had.
- Ask students to think about the word *grit* and how it relates to other words such as *tenacity, persistence, perseverance,* and *stick-to-it-iveness.* A great discussion starter might be: "Which is stronger, grit or perseverance?"
- What are some non-examples of grit?

Grit is important, but interests come first. Angela Duckworth responded to the question "Is it ever OK to quit?" The answer, of course, is yes!—Just don't quit on a hard day. What a powerful statement. Think of a time when you had a particularly challenging day: An annoyed parent showed up unannounced, your supervisor questioned a decision you made, or maybe outside of school you had a really lousy day on the tennis court. What kinds of thoughts may momentarily jump into your head? Thoughts like "I am going to change schools next year" or "I never liked tennis anyway, maybe I should try pickleball" It is not necessarily a bad idea to change schools during your career or try another sport—just don't make these kinds of decisions on a particularly bad day.

Finally, if you want to find out how "gritty" you are, try the Grit Scale. This ten-item scale can be found at https://angeladuckworth.com/grit-scale/.

This scale gives adults and middle and high school students an idea about how "gritty" they are. If they have a low score, then they can make a conscious effort to improve their ability to stick with tasks even after they have hit a wall. They can put in more practice time and can begin working toward being diligent about their actions—they might interview community or family members who have shown perseverance and demonstrated grit throughout their lives.

Productive Struggle

Productive struggle…sounds like an oxymoron, doesn't it? We want students to be in the zone of learning that causes that stretch or struggle—the challenge is that there is a fine line between productive struggle and frustration. Education authors Robyn Jackson and Claire Lambert described the difference between productive and destructive struggle (as cited in Allen, 2012).

Destructive struggle:

- Leads to frustration.
- Makes learning goals feel hazy and out of reach.

- Feels fruitless.
- Leaves students feeling abandoned.
- Creates a sense of inadequacy.

When a student is in a place of destructive struggle, he or she needs immediate intervention—the student may have run out of ideas/strategies for approaching the work. Sometimes their emotional regulation suffers.

Productive struggle:

- Leads to understanding.
- Makes learning goals feel attainable and effort seem worthwhile.
- Yields results.
- Leads students to feelings of empowerment and efficacy.
- Creates a sense of hope.

During productive struggle, students can wrestle with the task, try a variety of strategies, and eventually reach a solution. This is when kids develop perseverance and academic resiliency. It is fine to provide some guidance to students during productive struggle—just don't overhelp. Ask a question that might trigger a strategy to try or provide some scaffolding for support if needed. Guide students to ask questions that will trigger new thinking. Teach students about the importance of productive struggle.

For teachers, this two-minute video, *Teaching Habits that Promote Productive Struggle in Math* (Mind Research Institute, 2016; https://www.youtube.com/watch?v=HAd8n5x0LxU), is worth a watch. Even though it is focused on math, it can be applied across content areas. I particularly like the mention of creative problem solving and the Dos and Don'ts in the world of productive struggle, which can be seen in Table 5.1.

Remember those strategies for students who get stuck in Chapter 2:

- **Think aloud or self-talk** (metacognition)
- **Breaking material down into smaller chunks**

- **Taking a break—increases productivity and creativity**
- **Review previous feedback or examples**
- **Highlight to help focus**
- **Ask for help with a *specific* question** (*after* they have tried some strategies)

Many resources are available online that are specific to productive struggle in math; however, opportunities to struggle should not just be limited to math class. Provide opportunities across content areas for students to problem solve, wrestle with information, and think critically about content. Let students know that "struggle" is not a negative word—it just means they are learning.

Table 5.1
Dos and Don'ts for Productive Struggle

Don'ts	Dos
Don't always call on the kids who know the right answer.	Instead, model ways to be curious about incorrect answers.
Don't praise students for being smart (you already know that!).	Praise students for sticking with it and coming up with creative solutions.
Don't display A papers on your bulletin board.	Do show/display creative ways of thinking about a problem.
Don't just mark things right or wrong.	Do give informative feedback.
Don't have rigid time constraints.	Do allow time for students to tinker.

Note: These items were pulled from the video, Teaching Habits that Promote Productive Struggle in Math, developed by Mind Research Institute (2016) and accessible at https://www.youtube.com/watch?v=HAd8n5x0LxU.

Types of Mistakes

Eduardo Briceño, Cofounder of Mindset Works, has identified four common kinds of mistakes: the stretch mistakes, aha-moment mistakes, sloppy mistakes, and high-stakes mistakes. He described them as follows:

- **Stretch mistake.** These occur when we are doing something that is beyond our normal comfort level—when we are embracing challenge. It is good to make stretch mistakes: if we never make them, then we are likely risk-averse.
- **Aha-moment mistake.** This mistake happens when we achieve what we want to achieve, but then realize that we didn't have all of the information first. Briceño used the following as an example of this kind of mistake: "When we make incorrect assumptions: e.g. we try to help someone else, thinking that help is always welcome, but we find out that the person did not want help at that moment" (para. 13).
- **Sloppy mistake.** Sloppy mistakes are when we are doing something that we already know how to do, but because we are in a hurry or distracted, we make a mistake.
- **High-stakes mistake.** Life-threatening situations or performance-based mistakes fall into this category. A student who has worked his entire educational career so that he can get into a top Ivy League school and needs to do well on the SAT (performance-based) or a surgeon performing life-saving surgery are considered high-stakes events that can lead to high-stakes mistakes.

At the elementary level, teaching students the difference between stretch mistakes and sloppy mistakes may help them when they reflect on their process. Self-talk might go something like this:

> I made a lot of mistakes when I was trying to figure out that math problem. I really think that I made the mistake because I don't know how to do

three-digit division yet. It's OK though, because I tried and stretched my thinking.

Or:

I need to slow down and focus more when I do my assignments. I made some sloppy mistakes. I didn't show my teacher what I really understand.

Having students analyze the kinds of mistakes they make contributes to the reflective process, which is so important when developing a growth mindset. Other learning tasks for helping students learn to deal with and accept failure and mistakes can be found in Chapter 8.

Tom Kelley and David Kelley have this to say about dealing with a fear of failure: "Fear of failure holds us back from learning all sorts of new skills, from taking on risks, and from tackling new challenges" (p. 44). They continued,

You know you are going to drop the ball, make mistakes, and go in a wrong direction or two. But you come to accept that it's part of learning. And in doing so, you are able to remain confident that you are moving forward despite the setbacks. (p. 44)

Well said.

References

Allen, R. (2012). Support struggling students with academic rigor: A conversation with author and educator Robyn Jackson. *Education Update*, 54(8), 3–5. Retrieved from http://www.ascd .org/publications/newsletters/education-update/aug12/vol54 /num08/Support-Struggling-Students-with-Academic-Rigor .aspx.

Anderson, D. Elfman, Anthony, P., Macdougall, T., & Steve Bartek, E. S. (2007). *Meet The Robinsons*.

Blue, L. (2012). Motivation, not IQ, matters most for learning new math skills. *Time*. Retrieved from http://www.healthland .time.com/2012/12/26/motivation-not-iq-matters-most-for -learning-new-math-skills.

Briceño, E. (2015). *Mistakes are not all created equal*. Mindset Works. Retrieved from http://blog.mindsetworks.com/blog -page/home-blogs/entry/mistakes-are-not-all-created-equal.

Bruner, J. S. (1961). The act of discovery. *Harvard Educational Review*, *31*, 21–32.

Cyr, A. A., & Anderson, N. D. (2018, October). Learning from your mistakes: Does it matter if you're out in left foot, I mean field? *Memory*, *26*(9), 1281–1290. https://doi.org/10 .1080/09658211.2018.1464189. Epub 2018 Apr 16. PMID: 29659332.

Duckworth, A. (2016). *Grit: The power of passion and perseverance*. Scribner/Simon & Schuster.

Karou, K. (2016). *What do games have to do with productive struggle?* Retrieved from http://blog.mindresearch.org/blog/games-and -productive-struggle.

Kelley, T., & Kelley, D. (2013). *Creative confidence: Unleashing the creative potential within us all*. New York: Crown.

Moser, J., Shroder, H., Heeter, C., Moran, T., & Lee, Y. (2011). Mind your errors: Evidence for a neural mechanism linking growth mind-set to adaptive posterior adjustments. *Psychological Science*, *22*(12), 1484–1489. https://doi.org/10.1177/0956797611419520.

Pérez, A. B. (2012). Want to get into college? Learn to fail. *Education Week*, *31*(19), 23.

Pink, D. H. (2009). *Drive: The surprising truth about what motivates us*. New York: Riverhead.

The National Child Traumatic Stress Network (NCTSN) Resource. (2016). *Resilience and child traumatic stress*.

Tough, P. (2012). *How children succeed: Grit, curiosity, and the hidden power of character*. Boston, MA: Houghton Mifflin Harcourt.

Weiner, B. (1974). *Achievement motivation and attribution theory.* Morristown, NJ: General Learning Press.

Wormeli, R. (2011). Redos and retakes done right. *Education Leadership, 69*(3), 22–26.

CHAPTER 6

WHAT MESSAGES SHOULD PARENTS HEAR ABOUT GROWTH MINDSET?

"Can you explain the value of failure to my parents?"–Grade 11 student

Another stop along the path to a growth mindset school culture is to develop a plan for sharing information about growth mindset and neuroplasticity with parents. Even if a school or district is well on its way to developing a growth mindset environment, it is important to get parents educated so that children can hear a consistent message at home. In fact, it is because so many educators reached out begging for more resources for parents that the book *Mindsets for Parents: Strategies to Encourage Growth Mindsets in Kids* (updated in 2024) was born. It was written with the goal of being a partner book to this one—as schools travel along the journey to building a growth mindset environment, parents can learn to build a growth mindset home environment as well. Book study questions are included in the parent book so that parents can lead a book study and not require a school staff member to prepare for each gathering. The book is also available in Spanish as *Desarrollo De La Mentalidad Para Padres* (only

DOI: 10.4324/9781003406914-6

through Amazon) https://www.amazon.com/Desarrollo-Mentalidad -Mindset-Parents-Spanish/dp/169582234X/ref=sr_1_9?crid =2SS2ETCRUPKQ5&keywords=mary+cay+ricci &qid=1694902693&sprefix=mary+cay+ri%2Caps %2C271&sr=8-9 for Spanish-speaking families in your community. Also, I am happy to Zoom into one of the parent book club sessions—I love talking mindsets with parents!

Parents often struggle with the nature/nurture debate and at times attribute a child's success or lack of success to genetics. As clinical psychologist and author Oliver James (2008) stated, "Simply holding the belief that genes largely or wholly determine you or your children can be toxic" (para. 1). Parents, teachers, coaches, scout leaders, and other adult role models should never blame genetics for perceived capabilities. If any adult in a child's life communicates low expectations either verbally or nonverbally, then achievement can suffer.

A secondary outcome of educating parents about malleable intelligence is for themselves. According to Joel F. Wade (2012), author and life coach,

> Adults with growth oriented-mindsets are also more likely to engage in more challenging tasks, to persevere and to bounce back from adversity. Management teams with a growth-oriented mind-set outperform those with a trait-oriented mind-set...Also very interesting to note is that people with a growth-oriented mindset have a remarkably accurate assessment of their own performance and ability. Those with a fixed mindset have a remarkably *inaccurate* assessment of their own performance and ability. (para. 16–18)

Information about growth and fixed mindsets, encouraging resilience, neural pathways, and ways to praise their children are essential concepts that can be shared with parents. In doing so, children will hear a consistent message from adults in their lives that will significantly contribute to developing and maintaining an "I can do this" attitude. This can be done by posting information on the school website, social network sites, newsletter blurbs, principal coffee hours, and/or a parent information evening. (Sample newsletter blurbs in English and Spanish can be found in the Appendix.)

Building Resilience

A central message to communicate with parents is the importance of encouraging resilience in their children. Parents often overlook opportunities for helping children learn to adjust to situations when they are faced with adversity or lack of success. Saying to a child, "No wonder you did not do well on that test; you are always playing video games" or "You shouldn't have tried out for that team in the first place; you knew it would be a long shot" does not contribute to building resilience. Children will eventually try to avoid anything where they are not very sure that they will be successful rather than view the situation as a challenge to rise to. Some suggestions for building resilience in children include:

- *Use growth mindset praise.* Always praise a child's willingness to try, effort, patience, and practice. Do not attribute success to "being smart" or "being the best" but to hard work and perseverance.
- *Model flexibility.* There is an old adage, "We plan and God laughs" and as adults, we know how true that is. Children and teens, on the other hand, do not innately have the flexibility or adaptability to always handle a change of plans with grace. Being able to switch gears and change plans is important when building resilience in our children. One of the best things that we can do is to communicate that change is part of living life. Parents can model this for their children by taking a flexible mentality when things do not go their way. For example, if a parent plans a trip to a public pool, only to find it's actually closed for repairs, then he

or she could immediately model flexibility by selecting an alternate activity (or offering the kids some alternate activities to choose from). Taking this attitude in everyday life is important as well for parents, especially by not letting frustrating situations get the best of them.

- *Adopt a "glass half full" mentality in the home.* I remember that when my son was once facing a series of setbacks, he morphed into an almost constant "woe is me" mentality. I finally went to the kitchen cabinet, took out a glass, filled it halfway, then asked him, "Is this glass half full or half empty?" Given the situation he was in, he responded, "half empty." I asked, "Can you still drink from it? Does it still quench your thirst?" He responded that yes, it still could do both of those things. It was then that I made the analogy to the setbacks he was experiencing. Even during a hardship, we need to find positivity. A child with "hope" believes there can be a positive side to most situations. Parents also need to model a positive attitude, both verbally and non-verbally, when faced with their own setbacks. As far as my son goes, words were no longer necessary—all I had to do was get the glass out of the cabinet, fill it halfway, and set it on the table...he gets the message now.
- *Help children find their own niche.* A successful child is a confident child. Sometimes it means trying lots of different things before a child finds an area where she can thrive. This does not mean signing kids up for every lesson, sport, and club that comes along. It means providing opportunities for kids to experience a variety of things: cooking, scrap-booking, chess, stamp collecting, photography.

Teaching Parents About the Brain and Growth Mindsets

Just like many educators, parents typically do not have a conceptual understanding of what happens to the brain when learning new things. Educate parents about neural connections so that they can be aware of the importance of practice and persistence. Having parents participate in some of the student learning experiences that are included in Chapter 8 is also an effective and engaging practice. Students might even be encouraged to take home the materials they create as part of these learning tasks and share them with their parents, explaining to them how their brains work. *Ready-to-Use Resources for Mindsets in the Classroom* (Ricci, 2020) includes Ideas for Creating a Growth Mindset Environment at Home (pp. 67–70). These ideas are broken down into seven sections so that a different message can be sent home over seven weeks or seven months!

How Can Parents Communicate a Growth Mindset Message to Teachers?

Many parents naturally embrace a growth mindset mentality as simply a part of who they are themselves. Long before the advent of the terms "fixed mindset" and "growth mindset," some parents valued their child's effort and perseverance more than outcome. The conundrum that some of these parents face is that the message is not the same in school. Parents may want to focus on access when communicating with their child's school. If a parent feels that his or her child is not having access to challenging learning opportunities due to low expectations from the teacher, this should be discussed. It is possible that the student is right where they should be and that the teacher does provide opportunities through both ongoing assessment and student observation. However, it is also possible that a student is not provided with access to higher level learning experiences due to the teacher's perception of the child's intelligence, or perhaps the teacher does not have a differentiated classroom where those opportunities exist for any student. This is a more challenging situation for a parent, because communicating the concept of malleable intelligence is not really an appropriate conversation in a parent-teacher conference. However, conversations with the teachers could include some of the following:

- Christopher becomes much more engaged in learning when he feels challenged.
- I noticed that Christopher tends to do better on tasks that require critical thinking—have you noticed the same thing?
- Christopher loves a challenge. I noticed that he is much more motivated when faced with a challenge.
- What does Christopher need to do to have access to some higher-level thinking tasks?

Parents need to gauge the level of information to share based on the openness of the teacher and school administrator. At minimum, parents could stop by the principal's office or send an e-mail to a teacher or administrator with a message such as, "I found this really interesting book/article about mindsets and education that you also might find interesting." Parents can then provide the resources or link to them in an e-mail.

However, things do not always go as planned. For example, during a parent-teacher conference for one of my children, I mentioned to a science teacher that my child did not feel like she could be successful in science due in part to a previous negative experience in science. (The teacher told her that she was just not a science person.) Of course, my hope in sharing that information would be a response that would assure me that the teacher would send positive messages her way, help her in any way that he could, and praise all of the effort she puts forth. Well…not so much—his response was…wait for it…"Oh." Yes, just "Oh."

I then tried to engage him in a discussion about growth mindset. It was a one-sided discussion. I decided then that I would take matters into my own hands and really bump up my efforts in reminding my daughter about growth mindset and being able to succeed by persevering and requesting after-class help. I had talked to her many, many times about growth mindset, but now it was all about science. I realized a few things during this time—the most important being that students really needed to hear and feel the same message at school. Hearing it from a parent is just sometimes not enough. Students need teachers to believe in them as much as their parents do. Another lesson I learned is that if you talk to a 12-year-old about the same thing ad nauseam, then you will get "the hand"…as in the "Stop, I have heard this from you a thousand times before and it is not helping" hand gesture. In hindsight, I should have arranged another meeting with her teacher (with research on mindsets in hand) to make one last attempt to share the research about malleable intelligence and hopefully adjust his messaging to "effort" praise when responding to students' performance in science.

In situations where educators are just not "buying" the whole growth mindset/malleable intelligence research, all we can ask is for them to, at the very least, send messages that value effort. A principal once shared that he had a member of his staff who did not believe in the growth and fixed mindset research. She believed that she only ever had a few highly able students in her classroom each year. She remarked that most years the majority of her class was "average" and "below average." The principal asked her to continue to talk to her colleagues, gave her some additional resources on neuroplasticity and growth mindset, and offered to continue the discussion with her. But in the meantime, he asked her to do two things. First, he asked that she only use growth-oriented praise in her classroom, to praise what a student does, not who a student is—in other words, to focus on effort-based praise. Second, he asked this teacher to give all students opportunities to participate in higher-level learning experiences, even if she did not think the students were "ready" for it. Even though the teacher did not embrace growth mindset, she was asked to put some things in place that might positively affect her students. This is by no means the ideal, simply a bandage until the teacher organically sees the positive difference those few changes make. Because I have a growth mindset, I do believe that with effort, persistence, and the right people collaborating with her, she will eventually adopt growth mindset thinking.

Find Out What Parents Are Thinking

After a "Growth Mindset Parents Information Night" in one district, comments were gathered in order to capture what parents were thinking and planning based on the information they heard. Here are a few of the comments that they shared:

- "I am thinking about my son who achieves with minimal effort; now in seventh grade, material is becoming more difficult and more effort is required. I need to facilitate his growth mindset while maintaining his confidence. He likes having natural effortless perfection."
- "I don't encourage a growth mindset for math with my daughter, she says she doesn't like math and she isn't good at it. I don't disagree with her. I need to be more patient when things are difficult for her."
- "I need to really evaluate the way I praise my children. I need to have more self-controlled thinking before I speak. I am very proud of the efforts of all of my children but I am not sure they know it right now."

Gathering written feedback from parents after a growth mindset information session will give you data that will help inform your next session. A half sheet of paper with two simple statements "As a result of this session, I am thinking…" and "As a result of this session, I am planning…" can provide a lot of meaningful information.

You could also have parents take on a task similar to the one given to teachers in professional development sessions (see Chapter 2). Have them write down what they believe about intelligence before the workshop, then have them compare their answers after the workshop's conclusion. They can then apply what they've learned to how they might change their approaches when talking with their children.

In Staten Island, NY, Universal Literacy Coach, Sam (Sampurna) Rawal organized a Parent Book Club using the book *Mindsets for Parents* at Port Richmond School for Visionary Learning P.S. 68, New York City Public Schools. The school bought a set of books for the parents to use, and the group met once a week on Friday mornings after students were dropped off. Sam led discussions for the first few chapter sessions; she found videos and other resources that complemented each chapter and had great discussions with the parents (as well as a few grandparents). Beginning with Chapter 3, the parents partnered up and took turns leading the chapter discussions. They also found supplemental resources that they added to the discussions. I was lucky to be invited to one of the sessions, and I was blown away by the depth of discussion as well as the thoughtful questions that they posed. This was an excellent model for getting parents involved. My suggestion was that they continue with a new group of parents the following year and that a few of these parents become the leaders.

Providing information to parents about the importance of effort and persistence should be ongoing. Students can also be charged with interviewing their parents about their beliefs regarding intelligence. Children may, in fact, be the catalysts for helping their parents truly understand the malleability of the mind.

References

Ricci, M. C., & Lee, M. (2019, November 1). *Desarrollo De La Mentalidad Para Padres (Mindset for parents- Spanish edition): Estrategias para Fomentar la Mentalidad de Crecimiento en los Ninos*. Amazon Direct.

Ricci, M. C. (2020). *Ready to use resources for mindsets in the classroom: Everything educators need for building growth mindset learning communities* (2nd ed.). Routledge.

Wade, J. F. (2012, July 6). Editorial: Build a growth mindset. *The Daily Bell*. Retrieved from http://thedailybell.com/4055/Joel-F-Wade-Build-a-Growth-Mindset.

CHAPTER 7

CAN GIFTED EDUCATION AND GROWTH MINDSET THINKING COEXIST?

"I feel that if I have to try hard, I must not really be gifted."–Grade 7 student

Why does a book about mindsets include a chapter about "gifted" education you ask? Well, because an important issue is prevalent in many classrooms. The issue is that barriers to participation in advanced learning exist. One of the main reasons that barriers exist is due to a conception of giftedness that emphasizes and values only already-developed ability. If a school or system weighs already-developed ability, talent, or performance heavily when considering students for identification or participation in advanced programs, many students will be overlooked.

This process often fails to identify children who are less likely to live in a literacy-rich home and community where reading, writing, and language are understood to be critical for academic success. In many cases, otherwise capable children may not be able to demonstrate their advanced learning potential on a test or other performance assessments until after they have access to challenging curriculum and enriched learning opportunities. (Olszewski-Kubilius & Clarenbach, 2012, p. 9)

Think about that last phrase—"access to challenging curriculum and enriched learning opportunities." Are students in your school or district allowed these opportunities if they do not exhibit already-developed abilities? What are some ways that your school or district can allow for access to challenging instructional experiences for all students, especially those with potential or motivation to succeed?

The "Gifted" Label

Let's now think about the practice of labeling a child "Gifted." Doesn't telling a child that she is "Gifted" manifest a fixed mindset? This goes back to the importance of growth mindset praise. Growth mindset praise is about praising what the child does, not who the child is. We never want to say, "You are so smart," but saying, "You are Gifted" sends the same message—it says that the child has permanent traits and that those traits are being judged. Carol Dweck explained it this way:

To the extent that young people believe they simply have a gift that makes them intelligent or talented, they may not put in the work necessary to sustain that talent, moreover, the Gifted label that many students still receive, and that their parents relish, may turn some children into students who are overly cautious and challenge-avoidant lest they make mistakes and no longer merit the label. (as quoted in Horowitz, Subotnik, & Matthews, 2009, p. xii)

During a keynote address to Baltimore County, MD, educators in May 2012, Carol Dweck also shared that "Too much emphasis on who is Gifted creates kids who think they have to be infallible." Do the practice of identifying Gifted students and grouping them together contribute to a fixed mindset culture? What message do these practices send to the students deemed "Gifted" as well as the rest of the student population?

Former science teacher and university professor, Debbie Silver, author of *Fall Down 7 Times Get Up 8*, shares an experience that she had when her own son was identified as gifted. She felt proud when he was selected into a new gifted and talented program when he was in fourth grade. However, she observed that his participation in the program promoted a sense of entitlement that made him feel like he was smarter than everyone else:

> Occasionally, I overheard some of the kids in his Gifted class make disparaging remarks about their peers who were "not so bright." I think designers of G/T programs need to be heedful of mindsets and be cautious about encouraging growth rather than fixed mindsets in learners. (p. 89)

Silver went on to say that she felt that her son was not really able to enjoy the process of learning like most students due to feeling that he always had to "live up to the expectations about him always being the best—at everything. He mostly liked games that he could repeatedly win, and he quickly lost interest in areas where he was not immediately superior" (p. 89).

We have been having these discussions for a long time yet little has changed. Way back in October 2012, an edition of *Gifted Child Quarterly* contained the article "A Proposed Direction Forward for Gifted Education Based on Psychological Science." The authors (Subotnik, Olszewski-Kubilius, & Worrell, 2012) provided much food for thought regarding present practices in Gifted education; perhaps one of the more notable points mirrors a growth mindset belief: "What determines whether individuals are Gifted or not is not what they are but what they do" (p. 180). An homage to effort. The authors' interpretation of Giftedness continued, noting that, "There is growing literature on the importance of talent development, one can argue that Giftedness in children is probably best described as potential" (p. 180). The authors then described a continuum of development that begins with potential, grows to achievement (which is where many measure the "Giftedness"), and may or may not result in completely developed talents or, as the authors call it, "eminence." At each stage of development, instruction must be responsive to student needs. At the third stage, eminence, the learner must have opportunities to develop in his or her areas of strengths and areas of domain-specific abilities in unique ways. The authors suggest that these domain-specific strengths should be the areas that educators help develop further, even if this means introducing typical high school content in middle school and middle school content in elementary school.

Thinking about the research noted above, educators and parents must be careful about throwing around the Gifted and Talented (GT) label. If educators choose to use the term *Gifted*, it should be used in moderation. Perhaps when the child is an outlier within his or her age peer group and his or her instructional needs are so far beyond what is typically available that a very different instructional setting is needed, then the Gifted label may be applied.

Rather than overusing the term "Gifted," consider using other words or phrases such as "high-potential learners" or "highly motivated." Everyone has potential that needs to be nurtured, so consider using the word "potential" rather than the word "Gifted." Better yet, label the service that they receive—advanced academic program, enrichment cluster, advanced math, etc.—not the child. Also, it's important to note that the GT label becomes unimportant when students' instructional needs are being met consistently. Schools should adopt a differentiated, responsive instruction model as described in Chapter 3. Educators must work toward developing the talent in each and every child. If the needs of the students are being responded to within the course of instruction, then the need for a separate grouping of perceived GT students becomes less important.

Early Ability Grouping

Thankfully, the majority of school districts across the country do not begin to subjectively sort kids into separate, self-contained GT classes in every neighborhood school at the elementary level. Those that do are providing a disservice to their young students, both those in the "Gifted" class and those who are not. For the elementary students placed in a Gifted class, the situation perpetuates a fixed mindset—"I am smart, so I better not fail"—and in many cases, these students will avoid opportunities for intellectual risk-taking just as Debbie Silver described her fourth-grade son doing. What message does this structure send to the students not placed in the "Gifted" class?

Here's one example of the negative messages such a structure creates that I experienced. At a suburban school, three classes of grade 4 students were formed. Two of these classes were called "GT 4th Grade"; the final class was for all of the other students. Many savvy parents advocated for their students to be in a GT class and would do whatever they could to get on the "GT train." This district had a subjective process in place that did not include a cognitive assessment and weighed already developed ability heavily. The curriculum for this class was different from the on-level class in the four major content areas: reading, math, social studies, and science.

The parent of one of the students in the on-level class called the school system's GT office to share her daughter Rosa's experience in the on-level class. You might initially think that she was calling to get her child into the GT class; this was not the case, as the parent felt that an on-level class with differentiation was the appropriate placement for her daughter. Instead, the parent reported that, since the addition of the GT classes at fourth grade, Rosa had experienced many changes, particularly in the way she perceived what was expected of her. Rosa perceived that all of the smart kids must be in the other two classes and therefore she was not viewed as capable by the teachers in her school. Rosa's view (and perhaps this is shared by the teachers at her school) was that her teachers did not have very high expectations of her, as well as of the other students in her class. Rosa had been put on a track, and this track caused her to believe that she would not have access to different, more challenging instructional opportunities. For the students not grouped in the GT class, the message was loud and clear: "We do not expect much from you."

The parents of some "Gifted" students might argue that GT classes at the elementary level should not only exist, but also be exclusive due to perceptions that other students, who may not have yet developed their ability fully, may slow down their own children. They believe that policies and philosophies should be customized to those students who learn quickly, were born "smart," or have already "arrived." The GT policies in many school districts contribute to a fixed mindset mentality. These policies cause students, parents, and educators to believe that sorting kids at an early age is a good practice. It is not. However, **responding to the *instructional needs* of students at a young age is a non-negotiable practice**. Students need to continually be observed and evaluated through a lens of potential and possibilities. Educators must learn to recognize sparks and provide appropriate challenge. Children should have access to challenging instruction whenever they need it, at every grade level, in every content area. Early talent development experiences (Pre-K–2) that focus on building reasoning abilities and perseverance should be present in every setting.

> Responding to the *instructional needs* of students at a young age is a non-negotiable practice.

With that said, there are a few rare and uncommon young students who need an instructional setting that will allow them to further develop their gifts and talents. All students need an intellectual peer group. This is especially true when the student is an outlier in their abilities. Schools and districts do need to think about solutions for meeting the needs of students who lack an intellectual peer group in their neighborhood school. If it is a mid-sized or large district, then creation of a center for these outliers or highly able students should be considered. Perhaps beginning at grades 4 and 5, classrooms could be set up in a central location for those students whose needs cannot be met at their local school. These centers could provide what these students need instructionally and offer opportunities to develop domain-specific strengths more deeply. They could also provide an intellectual peer group and should be staffed with teachers with endorsement or certification in Gifted education.

In addition, the social and emotional needs of these students should be considered. It is imperative that a counselor be on staff who possesses the expertise in the social and emotional challenges that some of these outliers may face. These challenges include but are not limited to issues surrounding asynchronous development, overexcitabilities, perfectionism, and the adjustment of attending a nonfamiliar school. Those of us in the Gifted education field have espoused the importance of these unique social-emotional needs for years, but something interesting is happening right now in the field of Gifted education. I am beginning to read more studies and attend talks that suggest that perhaps some of these social-emotional behaviors—particularly overexcitabilities—may not be more common in cohorts of Gifted students. (One thing that should be noted is that Dabrowski's focus was on exceptional personality development, not Giftedness, when he developed the Theory of Positive Disintegration, often referred to as *overexcitabilities*.) I am going to sit back and pay attention (have a growth mindset) in the future to see where these studies lead us.

Wherever students are being educated, differentiated, responsive teaching strategies should be in place as a range of background knowledge, opportunities, and abilities exist in these settings as well. I remember receiving a phone call from a principal who was concerned about a child placed in a Gifted class. The child was falling behind, and the principal was considering removing him from the class. In order to gain more information, I began asking questions. One of the first questions that I asked was about differentiation—how the child did on preassessments. I also asked about the flexible grouping practices within the classroom. The principal responded with, "Didn't you hear me? I said it was a GT class. We don't differentiate in our GT classes." That response spoke volumes to me about how some educators view classes with highly able learners…they treat everyone the same.

At the elementary level, the majority of students' needs should be met in responsive, differentiated classrooms with flexible instructional groups. At the middle school level, the enrollment is typically larger and the probability of having an intellectual peer group is greater than elementary school; therefore, instructional choices should be available, such as "Standard" and "Advanced," "Accelerated," "Enriched," or "Honors" courses (note, no classes labeled "Gifted"). The expectation must exist that differentiated, responsive instruction will occur in all levels of courses. Look back to Chapter 3 for an overview of ways to create differentiated, responsive instruction in all classrooms.

If students believe that they will, with effort and perseverance, be successful in environments of challenging instruction, they are more likely to succeed. This is validated by findings in the NAGC *Unlocking Emergent Talent* report: "If students believe that they are welcome in advanced courses and teachers expect them to do well, they are more likely to bounce back from setbacks with increased effort and persistence" (Olszewski-Kubilius & Clarenbach, 2012, p. 17).

In June 2023, The National Working Group on Advanced Education released the report, *Building A Wider, More Diverse Pipeline of Advanced Learners*. This report focuses on traditionally underserved groups of children who cannot easily gain access to enriched and accelerated instruction. Even though this report is focused on students in the United States, many of the same challenges exist in other countries. The stage is set in this report with the following statement:

"The U.S. has been wasting a huge amount of human capital and squandering enormous amounts of human potential at the very moment we need more of it—and much of that wastage is among groups that have for far too long seen their opportunities limited and their potential squandered. We're talking about bright students, advanced learners, striving pupils, and those with high but untapped potential—especially those who are Black, Hispanic, Native American, low-income, or from otherwise marginalized backgrounds—whose educational needs aren't being satisfactorily met by our schools. The result is not just needless barriers to what racially underrepresented students and underserved young people from low-income backgrounds can learn and become, but also a pipeline of high-achieving students that is narrower and less diverse than we need it to be if America is to be competitive, prosperous, secure, equitable, and democratic in these challenging times." (pages 3 and 4)

The report provides many recommendations—one of the standouts is the following:

> **Err on the side of inclusion**, so that as many students can benefit as possible. The question should be whether a student has a need or would benefit from a particular service. When this isn't clear, schools should err on the side of giving students access to a more advanced group with intentional support. All of this avoids the problem of artificial and arbitrary scarcity.

Your Philosophy for Gifted Education

Reflect on the GT philosophy in your own school or school district. If you do not currently have a philosophy, consider building one that includes the following:

- A conception of Giftedness that emphasizes potential and possibilities. Use words and phrases like: access, potential, develop, nurture, motivation, *all* students, responsive, beliefs, talent development, and expectations.

- Curriculum development that embeds preassessment and formative assessment, as well as practices and strategies that develop and observe talent/potential, including critical and creative thinking.
- Identification processes for recognition of potential that are inclusive, use a variety of criteria, use local norms, are ongoing, and do not rely on referrals or nominations—data should be collected on *all* students, not just those who are referred or meet a certain test score. This process should embed direct instructional implications and not be a "stand-alone" process.
- Recognition of what students need and how these needs will be responded to both instructionally as well as social-emotionally. The "gifted" label is unimportant; the philosophy should be about responding to academic needs.
- Differentiated/responsive instruction that always allows for the possibility of enrichment and topic/content acceleration for all students. Remember, it is about access for all, not just those with a label.

A philosophy of Gifted education in a school or district that has adopted a growth mindset might sound like this:

Students in Pre-K–Grade 12 will have:

- Curriculum that embeds strategies that will develop potential, allow for development of talent, infuse 21st-century learning skills, and nurture creative and critical cognitive abilities in all students;
- Access to enriched and accelerated instructional opportunities for all students, specifically those with the capability, potential, and/or motivation to embrace the challenge;
- Instruction that is responsive to the needs of all students, which includes preassessment, curriculum compacting, flexible cluster grouping, rigorous enrichment and

acceleration experiences, and differentiated formative and summative assessments; and

- Educators who have adopted a belief system where they embrace a growth mindset about the malleability of the mind and have internalized neuroscience research that proves that everyone can get "smarter" with a proper instructional menu coupled with perseverance, effort, and motivation on the part of the learner.

For those students who are truly outliers:

- An instructional setting for those students who demonstrate profound, exceptional ability when compared with others of their age, experience, or environment and who have needs that cannot be met in a regular classroom setting.

Notice anything about the sample above? "Gifted" is not mentioned specifically at all. What has been developed is not just a Gifted philosophy, but a teaching and learning philosophy for all students that addresses differentiated, responsive instruction, curriculum development, and teacher beliefs/expectations. With the exception of the last bullet that addresses the need for an intellectual peer group for outliers, all of the other bullets are just about strong, differentiated, responsive instruction—something that every student is entitled to. The goal of every school or district is to develop an instructional philosophy that addresses the needs of our most advanced learners while at the same time allowing access to instruction for all learners.

References

Building a wider, more diverse pipeline of advanced learners: Final report of the national working group on advanced education. Thomas B. Fordham Institute (June 2023). Retrieved from https://fordhaminstitute.org/ national/research/building-wider-more-diverse-pipeline-advanced-learners.

Horowitz, F. D., Subotnik, R. F., & Matthews, D. J. (2009). *The development of giftedness and talent across the life span.* Washington, DC: American Psychological Association.

Olszewski-Kubilius, P., & Clarenbach, J. (2012, October). *Unlocking emergent talent: Supporting high achievement of low-income, high-ability students.* Washington, DC: National Association for Gifted Children. Retrieved from http://www.nagc.org/sites/default/files/Advocacy/Unlocking%20Emergent%20Talent.pdf.

Silver, D. (2012). *Fall down 7 times, get up 8: Teaching kids to succeed.* Thousand Oaks, CA: Corwin.

Subotnik, R. F., Olszewski-Kubilius, P., & Worrell, F. C. (2012). A proposed direction forward for Gifted education based on psychological science. *Gifted Child Quarterly, 56*(4), 176–188.

CHAPTER 8

WHAT ARE SOME WAYS TO HELP STUDENTS ADOPT A GROWTH MINDSET?

"I felt my brain growing when I was doing that game."–Grade 3 student

Have you ever heard of "Mind Brain Education" or "The Science of Learning"? What about The Center for Transformative Teaching & Learning (CTTL)? Yep, me nei-ther…that is, when I last updated this book in 2018. (By the way, this is the third update! Why bother to update a book three times, you may ask? Because we continually learn new things about our amazing brains and how that new informa-tion influences teaching and learning!)

These terms refer to fields of study that focus on the brain, how it learns, and how this information informs our teaching.

Just like many other advances in technology, the ways that scientists can "see" inside the learning brain through the use of imaging have made this field grow by leaps and bounds in the last several decades. The ideas presented throughout this

DOI: 10.4324/9781003406914-8

book have been greatly influenced by research about how the brain learns and grows. In some cases, it will confirm what you have already observed through watching students or your own children or grandchildren.

Studies estimate that the average human has 86,060,000,000 neurons (Harrigan & Commons, 2014)! There are 86,400 seconds in a day, so if you *could* count your neurons one by one, you would need to count more than a million neurons per second to finish counting in 24 hours. (That's an example that will make your head itch from the neurons connecting!) Helping to make an abstract "thing" like a neuron real to children is a challenge, but we believe that it is an important part (Ricci & Lee, 2024).

In fact, more and more studies and education organizations are communicating the importance of teaching students about their own brains. Increase of motivation, willingness to accept new challenges, and healthier reaction to failure are only a few of the benefits a child will experience when he or she understands how their brain works. With tight curriculum mapping and school districts' emphasis on consistent educational experiences among grade-level and content-area classes (as well as catching up from learning loss due to the pandemic), educators are losing the flexibility to "add on" anything more to an already very crowded curriculum and instruction plan. Therefore, resourcefulness and creativity are needed when looking for ways to embed neuroscience and growth mindset knowledge into the instructional day.

Please keep in mind that this is not a one-lesson experience—students need to be constantly reminded that they have the ability to grow their brains and that each and every brain has an elastic quality to it (neuroplasticity). It is very important how we use our brains. Therefore, we need to get creative about ways to teach and revisit the concept of malleable intelligence.

Begin to think about the subject area and grade level(s) that you teach. Where are the opportunities to introduce some basic brain education?

Learning Experiences in Neuroscience and Growth Mindset

On the following pages, ideas can be found for building a conceptual understanding of the brain, as well as fixed and growth mindset tasks for students. Following a responsive instruction model, each section will list several ideas for teachers to use with their students. Some can be used across many grade levels due to the open-endedness of the strategy or task. Others are learning tasks that are specific to grade levels. Use this as a menu and pick and choose learning opportunities that will be the most beneficial for your students.

Preview and Preassessment

As mentioned in Chapter 3, in order to plan for effective, differentiated instruction, we must first activate background knowledge and find out what students already know about the brain and how it functions.

Elementary Preview

The preassessment preview for elementary students might be as simple as a series of questions that initiate a discussion such as the following:

- Teacher points to his or her head and says:
- "Who knows what is in here?"
- "What do we use our brains for?"

Middle and High School Preview

Secondary students can actively take part in a discussion about the brain to help their teachers gauge their knowledge. Show students a picture of the brain and have a 2–3-minute discussion about the brain, allowing them to contribute information as the conversation flows.

Elementary Preassessment

Teachers should explain to the students that they would like to find out what they already know about the brain and how it functions. For example, you could say, "I am going to give you a paper, and I would like for you to do two things." Hold up a copy of the blank preassessment for the brain (see Figure 8.1) and ask the students, "Who can tell me what shape these dots are forming?" (anticipated response: head or face).

Distribute the preassessment and ask students to draw a picture of what they think their brains might look like inside the blank outline of the head. Then, students should write down anything that they know about their brain. Remind students that this is not for a grade; you are just interested in finding out what they already know.

After the students have completed the preassessments, review them, looking for patterns of responses. Common responses include:

- "My brain helps me think."
- "My brain makes me smart."

Also assess the students' drawings of the brain. Make generalizations about the students' baseline knowledge about the brain. Make note of any students who seem to have more than basic knowledge about the brain and plan for differentiation for these students (such as the completed assessments for Mike, Devin, and Alana in Figures 8.2 –8.4). Other students will have some knowledge of their brains but need more information about how the brain works. Some will simply be starting at the beginning and need much more instruction.

Middle and High School Preassessment

You can either give students a similar preassessment to the one in Figure 8.2 or students can simply jot down their ideas to the prompt: "Share everything that you know about the human brain."

Name _____ Date _____

Draw a picture of what you think your brain looks like.

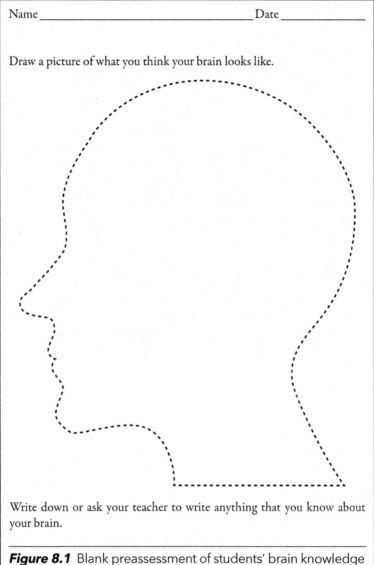

Write down or ask your teacher to write anything that you know about your brain.

_____

Figure 8.1 Blank preassessment of students' brain knowledge

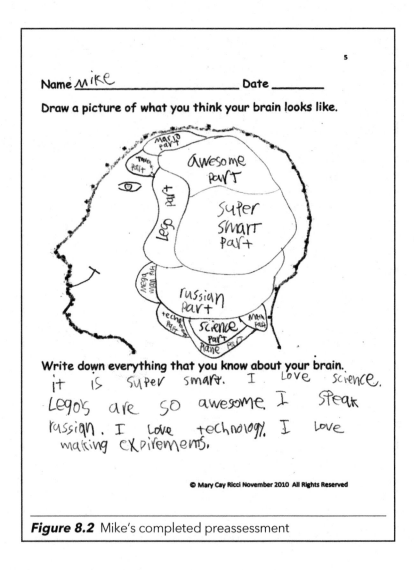

Name _Mike_ _____ Date _____

Draw a picture of what you think your brain looks like.

(labels in drawing:) macio part, twee part, leg part, awesome part, super smart part, new part, russian part, techno part, science part, math part, name PG

Write down everything that you know about your brain.

it is super smart. I love science. Legos are so awesome. I speak russian. I love technology. I love making experiments.

Figure 8.2 Mike's completed preassessment

Why Preassess? Will Students Really Know Much About the Brain?

At any grade level, the preassessment will serve as a way for teachers to find out just exactly where they need to begin. While preparing to give the above-mentioned preassessment to a group of Grade 3 students, their teacher remarked that it was probably

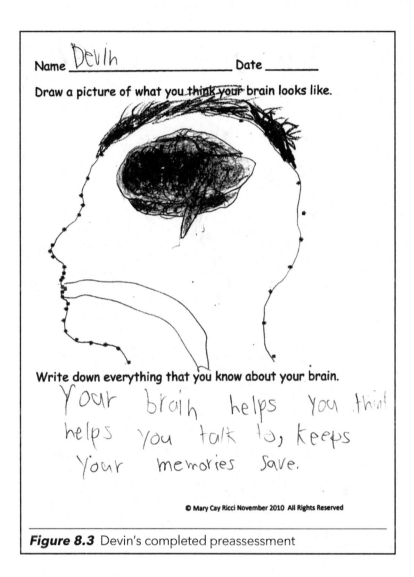

Name Devin _____ Date _____

Draw a picture of what you think your brain looks like.

Write down everything that you know about your brain.

Your brain helps you think helps you talk to, keeps your memories save.

Figure 8.3 Devin's completed preassessment

a waste of time because the students didn't know anything about the brain. In some cases, yes, the preassessment will demonstrate little to no understanding. I've had students respond simply with "My brain helps me think" coupled with a drawing of some scribbles or a spaghetti-like mass. Keep in mind that the purpose of a preassessment is so that you can match instruction to their

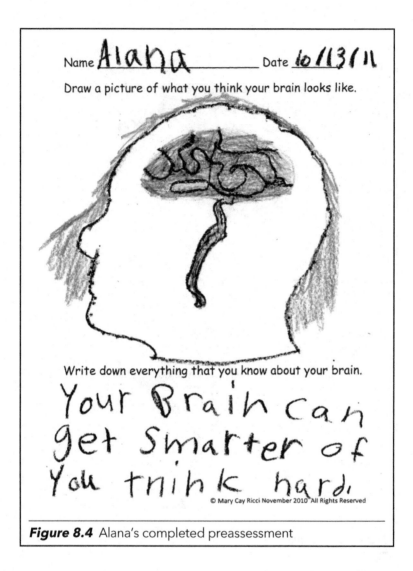

Name **Alana**   Date **10/13/11**

Draw a picture of what you think your brain looks like.

Write down everything that you know about your brain.

Your Brain can get Smarter of You think hard.

Figure 8.4 Alana's completed preassessment

needs—how will you know which students fall in the category of knowing much about their brain and which ones need more instruction without ever administering the preassessment? It's never a waste of time.

For example, through this process, many students have surfaced in all grade levels that show some understanding of brain function. Take a look at Vierra's brain preassessment in Figure 8.5.

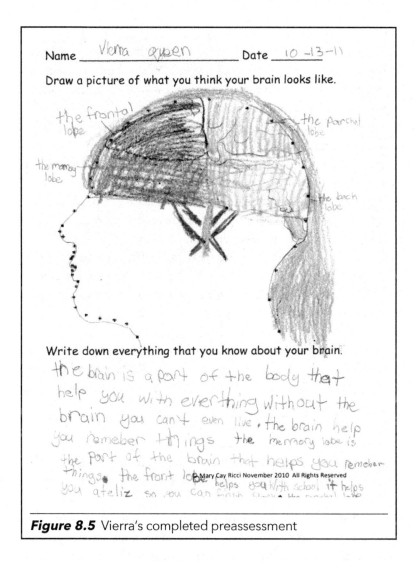

Name ___Vierra queen___ Date ___10-13-11___

Draw a picture of what you think your brain looks like.

the frontal lobe

the parchal lobe

the mamay lobe

the back lobe

Write down everything that you know about your brain.

the brain is a part of the body that help you with everthing without the brain you can't even live. the brain help you remeber things the memory lobe is the part of the brain that helps you remeber things. the front lobe helps you with school it helps you ateliz so you can finish

Figure 8.5 Vierra's completed preassessment

An interesting thing happened when I was visiting Vierra's third-grade classroom and administering the preassessment. Students were sitting at about six per table, and I was walking around observing when I noticed Vierra hunched over, pencil in hand, writing copiously on her paper. I stopped behind her for just a moment to take a look at what she was writing. No sooner had I stopped when one of the boys at the table announced: "Yes, look at her paper, she is the smart one." I assured him that he and all of the children at his table were working hard on the task. He thought about that for a minute and said, "Yeah, but she is still the smart one." I knew then that a lot of work was to be done to build a growth mindset culture in this classroom.

When I was evaluating the preassessments, Vierra's certainly did stand out, so I asked her teacher if I could speak to her for a few minutes. I complimented Vierra on her hard work and asked her where she had learned so much about the brain. She explained that her grandmother was a doctor, and she had learned from her.

I also questioned a first-grade student about a response that was shared on his preassessment. The child wrote that the brain was the place that "keeps the card in." After questioning the student, it was determined that he was referring to a memory card like those found in a digital camera or some video game devices—a place that stores all of your information. Talk about a 21st-century response!

Share with students a few common responses from the preassessment on the brain. For example, tell students "You worked hard on your 'brain task.' Many of you said that your brain helps you think!" Explain that they will be learning more about the brain, but first you would like to get their opinions on a few statements. Students can use "agree/disagree" signs or thumbs up/thumbs down to respond to the following three statements. These statements are adapted from Carol Dweck's Mindset Works (http://www.mindsetworks.com) workshop.

Tell students, "I am going to read and show you a few sentences. If you agree with them, then hold up your agree sign, and if you disagree, then hold up your disagree sign. Don't worry about what others are doing; I want to know what *you* think!" Take note of who agrees and disagrees with the following statements:

- Everyone can learn new things (Growth Mindset Belief).
- Some kids are born smarter than others (Fixed Mindset Belief).
- We can change how smart we are (Growth Mindset Belief).

We expect that all students should agree with the statement "Everyone can learn new things." What needs to be noted are the responses to "We can change how smart we are" and "Some kids are born smarter than others." If students agree with the latter statement, then chances are they have a fixed mindset when it comes to their own potential. As discussed in Chapter 1, we found that the older the child, the more likely they had a fixed mindset belief in some aspect of learning. You may also want to interview some students privately to find out about their mindset, particularly if you suspect the answer was not authentic. Or if you feel the need to make the reactions more anonymous, have students put their heads on their desks and then provide a thumbs up sign when they agree and a thumbs down when they disagree.

Once you've preassessed the students you're working with for both their knowledge of the brain and their thoughts on mindset, you can implement the sample learning tasks I describe in the next few sections.

Sample Learning Task #1: The Brain Is Like a Sponge (All Grade Levels)

"I know that my brain grows like a sponge and I have to exercise my brain like my body."—Grade 4 student

This learning task utilizes the Guess Box Strategy, based on the Concept Attainment Model developed by Jerome Bruner. This model is a teaching approach that helps students develop skills for *inductive* and *deductive* thinking. This can be done while learning content in any field in a constructive and meaningful way. A box in which the contents are unknown is a good vehicle for concept attainment and critical thinking—and very engaging for the students! Prior to the lesson, set up one wide column and one thin column on the smartboard or chart paper. At the top of the wide column, write "Attributes of a _____." At the top of the thinner column place a question mark (see Figure 8.6).

Attributes of a _____	
Attributes of a _____	?

Figure 8.6 Chart used for Guess Box Strategy

Let the students know that their task is to find out what is in the box. They may only ask questions that can be answered with a "yes" or a "no." Make it clear that the "no" answers are just as important as the "yes" answers because they give us valuable information about the item's attributes. As students learn about the item's attributes through their questioning, record all of the positive attributes on the chart paper. If you are unsure of how to respond to a question or you think the response would really mislead students, put the question under the "?" column. An example of this was when I had a clock in a Guess Box. A first-grade student asked me if the item in the box was a tool. Well, a clock is a tool, but I knew that if I said yes, then they would begin thinking of items like screwdrivers or hammers. So, I put the word "tool" under the "?" column and we talked about it at the end of the activity. There is no limit to the number of questions that the students can ask. In fact, it is when many of the students know what is in the box that the questioning becomes higher level and the teacher begins to recognize "sparks" in their students. Many teachers end the Guess Box strategy as soon as they think a few kids know what is in it; hence, students miss out on an opportunity to really conceptualize what the object represents.

It is very important to debrief and reflect on the Guess Box process after the item is revealed. Ask students the following:

- What question helped you (the most) to figure out what was in the box?
- Who asked that question? Why did you ask it?

Find out why students asked specific questions. Discuss with students which questions were important to them and why. What kind of information was gained from these questions?

- What are the three most valuable attributes? In other words, if we could only choose three of these words or phrases to describe this object, what would they be?

If students disagree, discuss the information that was gained with each attribute and come to a consensus. Strategies like Guess Box contribute to a growth mindset culture. Students who surface with well-thought-out questions can often be those students who may not shine in more traditional areas of school.

Once students are familiar with the process of the Guess Box strategy, use it to facilitate new learning about the brain using the *Guess Box: Let's Get Your Brain Working!* lesson described in the next section.

Guess Box: Let's Get Your Brain Working!

Put a dry, flat sponge in a guess box. If possible, use a flattened "pop up" sponge that expands or changes shape when it gets wet. Set up the chart paper with two columns: "Attributes of a _____ " and a question mark. Tell the students:

> *This is something that comes in a lot of different colors so you do not have to ask any questions about color.* (You may want to add that many are yellow.) For younger students you may also want to add the following clue: *This is something that you might use when you clean.*

Then allow the children to ask questions to try to determine what's in the box. After students have asked many questions about the mystery object in the box, the chart should list the attributes that helped students come to the conclusion that a sponge was in the

Kindergarten	First Grade	Second Grade
Use it to clean	Use it to clean	Use it to clean
Many are yellow	It is usually a	It is usually a rectan-
It is in your house	rectangle	gular prism
Usually in the	You can find it in the	Use it to wash dishes
bathroom	kitchen	It has six faces
Usually in the kitchen	It can clean a hard	Use it to clean the
It is squishy	floor	floor
It can be hard	A person makes it	It is squishy
It is usually a	work	It has holes in it
rectangle	It is sometimes soft	Use it with soap
It can get wet	You can rip it	You need to wet it
It feels bumpy	You can use it to wipe	
You can dry it	It needs water	
	You can use it with	
	cleaning spray	

Figure 8.7 Attributes of a Sponge–Guess Box

box. Figure 8.7 includes examples of the charts from kindergarten, first-, and second-grade classrooms I worked with. These attributes are listed as a result of the questions that the students asked.

After students determine that a sponge is in the box and they debrief the process they used to get there, pose this question: *How is your brain like a sponge?* Ask students to think about things that are the same when thinking about a sponge and a brain. Actual student responses have included:

- They are both pink.
- They are both squishy.
- They both grow.
- They both absorb.

Now, set up the following scenario for students:

> *Let's take a look at our sponge again. I am putting it in this jar, and I am going to slowly add water to it. Now it is time to use your imagination: Let's*

pretend that the sponge is your brain and the water represents all of the new things you learn every day. What do you think will happen to your brain when you add all of the new things that you learn?

Slowly pour water over the sponge. The students will see how the sponge begins to grow and absorb the water. Tell them, *Every time you work hard and learn something new, your brain grows and gets stronger. The sponge is bigger and will now work better since it is wet.* Students can then observe what happens to the sponge over several days without water: It begins to dry and shrivel. Relate this to what happens to a brain when it is not being challenged.

Sample Learning Task #2: Building a Neural Network

"If work gets hard, I just imagine neurons in my brain trying to connect."—Grade 5 student

Several ideas are provided below to help students build a conceptual understanding of what happens in the brain when they learn. These explanations also help students visualize the neural connections that are made and strengthened with learning, practice, and mastery.

Before you share these learning experiences, give students some background on how the brain works, telling them, *Inside the brain we all have brain cells called neurons. We have billions of neurons; some connect to each other, and some are just sort of floating around.* Show them a picture or diagram of a neuron, like the one in Figure 8.8. Ask students to think about what might cause these neurons to connect with each other. Here are a few sample learning experiences that can help you teach students this concept:

1. *Learning Experience #1: Students Become Neurons.*
   - Ask for three to five students to volunteer to be neurons. With elementary and middle school students, you can have

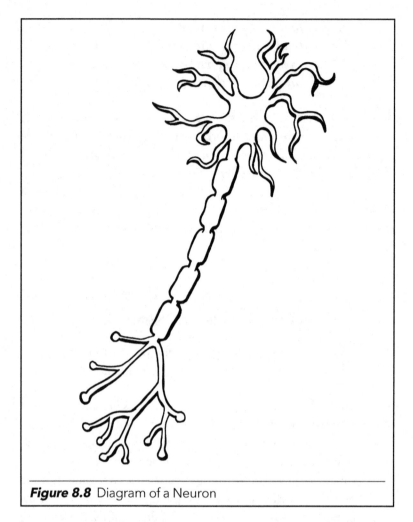

Figure 8.8 Diagram of a Neuron

them hold a picture of a neuron or hang a cardstock neuron around their necks.

- Ask the students if someone could share something new that he or she has learned recently. Responses might include multiplication, a foreign language, knitting, a sport, and so on. For illustrative purposes, we will choose Sam's response. Sam shared that he just learned how to divide in math class. Announce that this group of neurons now represents part of Sam's brain.

- Take a thin piece of thread and ask two of the student neurons to connect using this thread, with each of them holding one end. This thin connection will represent division. Explain to the students that Sam is just beginning to learn how to divide, so this is a connection that is not yet strong.

- Ask Sam if there is something that he has learned and that he is getting better at but still might need some practice. In this case, let's say that Sam responds with "multiplication." At that point, two of the student neurons can connect using a thicker string such as a piece of yarn. This represents a better understanding of multiplication than division, but it is not yet at a mastery level.

- Then propose the following scenario: *Let's look at Sam's division connection: It is represented by a thin piece of thread, but what will happen to this connection after Sam has more experience learning about and practicing division? Let's say that Sam persists and puts forth a lot of effort and eventually becomes an expert in division. How will this connection change?* At this point demonstrate how this thin thread of a connection is replaced with a strong, thick rope (Macramé cording or a piece of rope works well here). See Figures 8.9 and 8.10 for examples of how this lesson was implemented in two classrooms.

- What if, instead, Sam decides that division is just too hard for him and he gives up? What will happen to this connection? (It will stay a weak connection or disconnect entirely.)

- Ask students to think of a time when they felt frustrated learning something new. Ask them to visualize their neurons making stronger connections every time they push through the challenge and master new learning. Tell them to think about these neural connections when they are faced with a challenge.

- You may also ask students to draw their strong and "not yet" neural connections. Draw a rough shape of the brain on a piece of paper and ask students to think about things they understand and are very good at as well as things that they are

Figure 8.9 Students in Betsy Book's first grade class at Randallstown Elementary School in Maryland demonstrate neural connections

Figure 8.10 Grade 1 students in Farrah Connelly's class discuss which connections are strong (thick rope) and which connections represent new learning (thin piece of thread)

Figure 8.11 Illustration of neurons making a connection
Source: Nothing You Can't Do! The Secret Power of Growth Mindsets (Ricci 2018)

just learning, but "not yet" understanding fully. Take a look at Figure 8.12. Kamaren's brain shows very strong neural connections for math, spelling, and riding his dirt bike. He explained, however, that his strongest connection is "bugging my mother"—he felt he was very good at that!

2. *Learning Experience #2: Road Map.* Make an analogy to destinations and roads to explain the connection between neurons and the brain. For example, draw a picture of the school on the board, then ask students how they might get from the school to their home, to the store, to a gas station, and so on. Then show how they can move from that location to another one. Each location (neuron) has a connection or path to another destination. You can use a map like the one in Figure 8.20 to help you demonstrate this to your class. Tell students:

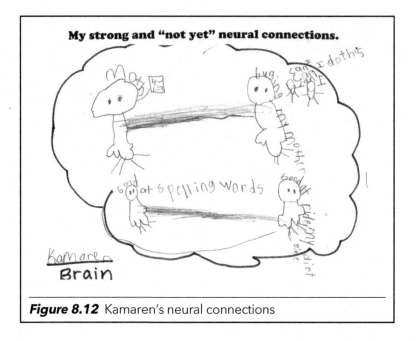

My strong and "not yet" neural connections.

Figure 8.12 Kamaren's neural connections

"Some have strong connections to a lot of different locations, and others are weaker because you don't travel to that particular destination often. When you learn a new route, or a new road is built, this makes new connections. Neurons work in a similar way. They make hundreds of connections. The more you learn, the more connections are made. The more they are traveled, the stronger the learning."

3. *Learning Experience #3: Visualization.* Ask students to visualize walking through an unexplored forest. You can use this script as you walk them through their visualization session:

> *There are no paths, no plants that have been trampled on, nothing to lead the way. A new neural pathway is like walking through an unexplored forest for the first time. The more frequently the path is used, the fewer the barriers and obstacles that stand in the way. Eventually a clear path is created. That clear path represents a clear understanding of what you are learning to do.*

Figure 8.13 A map that can help students visualize neural pathways

4. *Learning Experience #4: Use Manipulatives.* Elementary classrooms can order plushy neurons from http://www.giantmicrobes.com. These cute brain cells can be used to demonstrate neural connections that are made during learning. Primary students particularly like demonstrating brain activity using these furry brain cells (on a recent grade 2 classroom visit, I met Ned and Nellie Neuron ☺.) Kindergarten students can also join hands to demonstrate neural connections.

5. *Learning Experience #5: Use Technology to Show Students' Neurons in Action.* Many videos exist online that demonstrate neural connections. A good resource is the website Neuroscience for Kids, which was created with the support of a Science Education Partnership Award from the National Center for Research Resources. The site can be found at https://faculty.washington.edu/chudler/neurok .html

You may also want to show them this 25-second video showing neurons connecting—it's actually a Twitter (X) post—very cool! https://twitter.com/slava__bobrov/status/1620761884570836992

The older the students are, the more content can be added about learning and the brain. For example, once students have an understanding of neural connections, an introduction of dendrites and synapses would be a logical next step. A dendrite is a branch-like projection off of a neuron that receives incoming messages from other neurons. A synapse allows a neuron to pass a signal to another neuron. After a discussion or demonstration about creating neural pathways, ask students to complete a formative assessment in order to help you gauge their understanding. Simply give each child a blank piece of paper and ask the students to draw or write about all of the things they have learned about the brain. Teachers review formative assessments to check for understanding. If necessary, work with students who have not conceptualized the idea of the connections of neurons and approach the instruction in a new way.

Sample Learning Task #3: The Brain Is Like a Muscle

"What? You mean I can exercise my brain like a muscle?"—Grade 7 student

Explain to the students that the brain is like a muscle—the more you use it, the stronger it gets. This is usually an easy concept for students to comprehend, especially when you use a demonstration process like the following:

- Show students a two-pound hand weight. (Older students may want to use a five-pound weight.) Ask a student to demonstrate how someone might use this weight to exercise. Ask the following question: *If I ask someone to exercise every day with this weight, after a lot of practice what will happen to their arm muscle?* Actual student responses I've heard have included: "They will get stronger," "They will make a strong muscle," and "It will get easier to do." Explain to the students that the more they practice using the weight, the easier it gets. Ask students why this will happen. Students may answer with something like, "Because they practiced every day, they learned how to do it." Continue to question students, "If they want more of a challenge and want to continue to build more muscle, what should they do?"

- Then, show students a three-pound weight (older students may want to use a ten0-pound weight) and hand it to the student who is giving the demonstration. Ask them how the weight feels compared to the two-pound weight. Acknowledge that it is heavier, but with practice, it will become easier to lift. The teacher could further explain the concept by using an example of something students learned earlier in the year and comparing it to something they are learning now. One first-grade student explained it this way: "The lighter weight is like when you learned to count to ten. You practiced until it became easy. The heavier weight is like learning to count to 100! It is a little harder, but if you practice, it gets easier."

- Ask students to think about how practicing with two different-sized weights is like a brain. Explain that we need to keep trying to learn new things to help our brain get really strong! The neurons make more connections and make our brain stronger just like arms make more muscles from the weights. Tell students, *Even when we face something really hard or challenging, think about all of those new connections your brain is making and how much stronger it is getting!*

Another way to supplement their learning is by the use of the picture book *Your Fantastic Elastic Brain: Stretch It, Shape It* (2010) by JoAnn Deak when you're explaining these concepts to elementary students. This book explains the various functions of the brain, how it grows and connects, and what the different parts of the brain look like and do. I recently discovered another book by Deak, *Good Night to Your Fantastic, Elastic Brain: A Growth Mindset Book for Kids about the Amazing Things your Fantastic Elastic Brain Does after You Say Good Night* (2022). Need one for older kids? Well, JoAnn Deak has it covered in *The Owner's Manual for Driving Your Adolescent Brain* (2013).

After the demonstration, conduct a formative assessment by asking students to recall everything that they have learned about the brain so far. Chart their responses. The main ideas you will want to capture include:

- Your brain can grow and get stronger.
- Neurons in your brain make new pathways or connections when you learn.
- Your brain is like a muscle.
- Exercise (learning and embracing challenge) is good for your brain.
- When you learn something that is at first challenging, keep practicing! This helps your brain get stronger.

Sample Learning Task #4: Taking Care of Your Brain

–Explain to the students that it is also very important that your brain gets enough sleep. Studies have shown that lack of sleep affects memory and increases the time it takes to perform certain tasks (that goes for us as well!). Have each student generate a plan that will make sure that they get enough sleep each night. The plan may include turning off electronics an hour before bed, pulling shade/ curtains, putting on white noise, and most importantly, getting to bed at a time when they will get a good night's sleep (9–11 hours per night for school-age kids).

Older students can research foods that are considered super brain foods. For younger students, explain that certain foods also have an effect on the way the brain functions. Ask students if they know of any foods that are super brain foods. Using pictures or plastic foods, show students a few of the best brain foods. One at a time, reveal and discuss the following: eggs, fish, nuts, berries, and bananas. It is important to note that students should eat these foods, as well as other healthy foods, routinely, not just on the morning of a test! As one fifth-grade student announced after this discussion, "Before my test tomorrow, I am going to have a crab omelette with blueberries, bananas, and nuts on the side!" Comments like these are a great way to show the importance of taking care of your brain at all times. Point out that it is also important for our brains to drink lots of water and stay hydrated.

Explain to students that physical exercise can also increase brain power. Exercise sends a higher level of oxygen to the brain. This extra oxygen makes the brain more alert. When people exercise on a regular basis, they typically can increase their ability to remember new information and will do better academically.

Sample Learning Task #5: Collection Strategy

In this learning task, a collection of objects assembled around a specific concept is used to help students develop classification strategies, analyze attributes of objects, and discover relationships between items. This strategy is based on Jerome Bruner's Concept Formation model and is also a powerful tool for developing critical thinking. There are two kinds of collections: *serial* and *revealed*. In a revealed collection, all objects are displayed at the same time. If the common link between the objects is obvious, a revealed collection works well. The focus would be on finding similarities and differences within the group. A set of toy animals or models of transportation that share a connection would make an appropriate revealed collection. A serial collection is used when items are displayed one at a time. After each item, the teacher records students' predictions on index cards as to what the common concept might be for all objects in the collection. With each item that is presented, remove the cards with concepts that no longer work. The last item in this collection is the validator, which should help solidify the common concept of the collection. It is possible that many ideas remain that could work to describe the concept presented. That is fine. Just share with the students what you were thinking of. Perhaps they can think of some additional items that would fit in the collection.

When doing this strategy with students, I like to present the following items in this specific, brain-oriented collection:

- dollhouse bed, pillow, or another symbol of sleep
- toy bike, ice skate , ball, or an athletic shoe to represent exercise
- banana
- bottle of water
- nuts (picture or plastic if there are allergies)
- egg
- fish (plastic or a picture)
- a science book
- a picture of a school or something to represent a classroom

The order of each item revealed is very purposeful. After each item, the teacher records students' predictions on index cards or sticky notes as to what the collection may be focused on. After each item is revealed, the teacher reviews all of the predictions that have already been generated. Students determine if the card/sticky note should stay in as a possibility or be removed. If any student can justify why it should stay in, leave it in. You can also bring back any previous categories if a student discovers a common attribute that was not previously mentioned.

The common concept that is being formed in the collection listed above is "things that are good for your brain" such as sleep, exercise, brain foods, water (hydration), reading, and learning. After the collection is complete, debrief the process of the collection by asking students, "After I took out each object, what were you think-ing/what was your brain doing?" Let students know that they just exercised their brains and made them stronger by coming up with all of these ideas (point to category cards). Explain to the students that it does not matter if an idea was the same as the teacher's; they made their brain stronger just by thinking about the connections among the items in the collection!

Review with the students all of the different ways that we can help ourselves become smarter (point to the collection). Tell them, "It is important to always believe that if we try hard, our brains can grow." Discuss the meaning of the word *effort* and ask students to share specific examples of the ways that they put forth productive effort.

Introducing Growth Mindset Terminology

After completing some or all of the preliminary lessons to build students' knowledge of how their brains work, you're ready to introduce them to the ideas behind what makes a growth mindset. Explain to the students that if we always believe that with productive effort, perseverance, and resilience we can learn and become smarter, then we will have a growth mindset. Show students the Growth Mindset Poster found in Figure 8.14.

After students understand what growth mindset means, introduce them to the concept of a fixed mindset. Tell students,

> *Sometimes, people do not believe that they can get smarter with effort. These people have a fixed mindset. So if you hear yourself saying, "I am not very good at math or reading or sports," that is a fixed mindset. Instead say: "Math is sometimes hard for me, so that means I need to always try harder and practice to make my brain stronger in math".*

Using direct examples of the types of things people with a fixed mindset tell themselves (like those shown above) is very helpful for students to understand when they may have had a fixed mindset about a task or event in the past. Encourage students to think about examples of growth and fixed mindsets in their own lives and in the lives of the characters in books, movies, and TV shows they enjoy.

Figure 8.14 Growth Mindset Poster

Next, share with the students that they should always strive to have a growth mindset. Tell them:

> *Sometimes we feel like we can't learn something new, like a new video game or how to work a new cell phone or how to speak another language, but then we can remind ourselves to have a growth mindset and realize that if we stay motivated, practice, and use strategies that help us learn, we can learn to do almost anything! In our classroom, we will be working toward having a growth mindset community every day. Sometimes I may point to our growth mindset poster to remind you to persevere. Each one of us will always persevere and remind ourselves that we need to embrace challenges.*

Embedding Growth Mindset into Curricula

One of the most effective ways to encourage growth mindset thinking is through literature. Take a look at the books and anthologies in your curriculum that are used. Identify the text pieces that could be used to demonstrate growth and/or fixed mindset thinking—tenacity, grit, resilience, persistence, perseverance, work ethic, optimism, goal setting, etc.

Literature is a very effective way to embed growth mindset principles. Identify and discuss books that demonstrate perseverance, persistence, and effort:

- *The Little Engine That Could* by Watty Piper—after a class discussion about the book, pose these questions, "What if the Little Engine decided that he couldn't instead of could? How would the story change?" "What would happen if he said 'I don't think I can' instead of 'I think I can'?"
- *Wilma Unlimited: How Wilma Rudolph Became the World's Fastest Woman* by Kathleen Krull—this is the story of runner Wilma Rudolph. Focus first on the word in the title, "Unlimited." Ask students to predict why the author chose the title. Then, after the book is read, discuss the title once more, focusing on Wilma Rudolph's perseverance.

- *Amazing Grace* by Mary Hoffman—Grace wants to play Peter Pan in the school play but is facing resistance; discuss what Grace does to persevere.
- *Butterflies for Kiri* by Cathryn Falwell—Kiri practices and perseveres until she is successful with origami.

If you have the budget for additional books or library purchases, *Ready to Use Resources for Mindsets in the Classroom* (2020 version) provides a list of 100 picture books and 50 extended texts along with the author's name, recommended grade level (although I am a fan of using picture books at every level), date published, and whether the character or story demonstrates a fixed mindset, growth mindset, or both. I also added a column that refers to any evidence from the story that supports the mindset. The inclusion of some growth mindset questions that could be asked about the text rounds out the table. Many question possibilities exist for each book—the questions on the chart are just a few examples in order to begin a discussion about mindsets.

A children's book for teaching and conceptualizing mindsets for students ages 9 to 13ish is *Nothing You Can't Do! The Secret Power of a Growth Mindset* (Ricci, 2018) This can be used in any class or group learning about mindsets: counseling group, study skills class, middle school transition course, Reading Language Arts class as a non-fiction text reading or a recommended summer reading book.

Additionally, during a Biography Unit, think of biographies of people who demonstrate a growth mindset. Students can be encouraged to choose to read about people who model perseverance, resiliency, optimism, and work ethic. Some of those people include: Susan B. Anthony, Cesar Chavez, Misty Copeland, Walt Disney, Albert Einstein, Milton Hershey, Steve Jobs, Nelson Mandela, Sonia Sotomayor, Harriet Tubman, and Wilma Rudolph.

We can also work to build a conceptual understanding of these words (which can be added to vocabulary): tenacity, grit, perseverance, persistence, stick-to-it-iveness, determination, stamina, endurance, diligence, drive, resiliency.

Science

Chances are that almost every scientist and researcher that your students learn about has demonstrated a growth mindset. Persistence and tenacity are important when developing experiments and doing research. Make sure that this, along with the importance of learning from failure, are part of your discussions. Additionally, science is the perfect place to dive deeper into those neuroscience lessons to teach kids about the brain…specifically neural connections. During a health class, be sure to include discussion and discovery surrounding food and sleep habits that promote healthy brains.

Social Studies

Take a look at your Social Studies Curriculum and highlight historians who have demonstrated a growth mindset. Identify communities around the world that have had to rebuild due to war, weather, financial challenges.

The Arts

I find it interesting that almost every time I ask a group of people this question, "What areas of your life do you find yourself having fixed mindset thoughts? Those activities where you say, you just can't do them…what are those areas for you?" In most cases, at least one person says "I can't draw" or "I am a terrible singer." The arts seem to be an area where fixed mindset thinking is prevalent. Let students know that everyone can show growth in music, visual arts, and performance arts…with deliberate practice. Identify artists who overcame challenges throughout their lives and perhaps a few painters who were never recognized for their art, in fact were taunted yet continued to paint what are now considered masterpieces.

Physical Education (PE)

Howard County Maryland Elementary Phys Ed Teacher, Suzy Serpico, consistently communicates growth mindset messages to her students. She shares:

Learning about Growth Mindset has helped me both personally and professionally. Reflecting on 20 years as a competitive athlete, I realize that I owe a great deal of my success to a Growth Mindset. Implementing Growth Mindset in my elementary Physical Education instruction has been successful and rewarding. Many children compare their athletic skills to others and feel they don't measure up. Educating them on the skills and vocabulary of Growth Mindset has increased their confidence, their determination, their perseverance, and often, their performance. I wholeheartedly endorse the use of Growth Mindset in Physical Education programs. (Ricci, 2018)

Games That Build Perseverance

Through the Critical Thinking Growth Mindset project discussed in Chapter 4, it was discovered that when students engage in reasoning games that grow more complex as they play, they build perseverance for learning tasks. Games made by ThinkFun that progressively grow more challenging, thus building perseverance, include ShapeOmetry, Chocolate Fix, Brick by Brick, Shape by Shape, Rush Hour and Rush Hour Jr., Swish and Swish Jr., and Block by Block. (Check the Thinkfun website since some of these games may have been discontinued.) It is amazing to witness students who typically give up persevering and try to get to the next level of challenge. These can be easily justified for classroom use for several reasons. The first is that perseverance is one of the Common Core State Standards for Mathematical Practice: "Make sense of problems and persevere in solving them." Another justification is that these games also build reasoning processes, which is an important skill for life and test-taking. They can be used as centers or anchor activities and always be available before and after school, as well as during indoor recess time for elementary students.

Teaching Perseverance and Resiliency Through Makerspaces

Makerspaces are wonderful innovation hubs that are popping up in schools across the world—they are places where students can problem solve, explore, innovate, persevere, and learn from struggle and failure. The spaces are stocked with "stuff" that students can manipulate, create, and innovate. Some of the materials you might see in makerspaces include felt, coin cell batteries, wire, light bulbs, conductive thread, and copper tape; in more sophisticated makerspaces, you may see power tools, 3-D printers, microprocessors, and sewing machines. However, these spaces are not about the "stuff": Makerspaces are places where students are guided, a place where teachers should take a back seat and allow students to experiment. A perfect environment for cultivating a growth mindset.

I had the idea of establishing makerspaces in about 100 elementary schools in Prince Georges County, Maryland, where I was Supervisor of Advanced and Enriched Instruction. Not only would

Figure 8.15 Growth mindset during Makerspace!

Source: Nothing You Can't Do! The Secret Power of Growth Mindsets (Ricci 2018)

these spaces provide opportunities for students to think critically and problem-solve, but they would also provide a wonderful opportunity to learn about growth mindset. Although our office had deep knowledge of best instructional practices for advanced learners, we lacked the hands-on makerspace experience. I knew that our office could not do this alone so I reached out to two other departments in our district: Office of Library Media Services and Media Arts-Arts Integration Office. Lucky for everyone, this newly formed collaboration included two educators who eat, speak, and breathe makerspaces: Susan Brown, Instructional Specialist, Office of Library Media Services, and Barbara Liedahl, Instructional Specialist of Media Arts (who were also rock stars on the makerspace conference circuit). Together, our three offices planned and developed an inquiry-based makerspace enrichment program. The first part of the year would focus on paper circuits, and the last part of the year would focus on e-textiles. The initial participants in the spaces would be fourth- and fifth-grade high-potential and advanced students. The new program would replace a pull-out enrichment program that these students had previously participated in for two hours each week.

In addition to the tinkering and making that the students would participate in, growth mindset would be embedded. Students would make pipe cleaner neurons and learn about the brain and neural networks, and they would learn that mistakes are all part of the process. Books like *Rosie Revere, Engineer*, and *The Most Magnificent Thing* were also part of the program. Learning experiences were designed to build the concept of circuitry through making and literature. Students used a digital reflection journal at the end of each session—this journal included prompts that asked students to focus on the process and struggle that they went through, not the end product.

Susan and Barbara worked with the pull-out teachers who requested additional support. The pull-out teachers often had other roles to wear in the school, such as media specialists, reading teachers, counselors, and testing coordinators, as the schools had the flexibility to choose who would facilitate this program. Barbara and Susan also had the opportunity to work with students when they did school visits and shared the following with me:

> We were working with a group of advanced fourth-and fifth-grade students; the students had been using paper templates to create copper circuits to illuminate a light emitting diode (LED). We decided that if they were really going to learn this, we needed to take away the templates, and let them practice by creating their own circuit. They were asked to design their own circuit, then bring the drawing to us, showing us how much copper tape they would need to make this circuit work. Some struggled. Measuring wasn't easy, making sure that the circuit worked wasn't easy, but they were determined. Once they were finished, we had them write about what they had done.

The story that they shared is a wonderful example of allowing students to take ownership of the learning and to overcome the struggles that they may face. Kevin, a student at James McHenry Elementary School in Lanham, MD, shared this after the lesson:

> Today's lesson was astonishing. I was able to create my own circuit and not listen to other people on what I had to do. I really liked it because my circuit was challenging and not the easy circuits that they make us do. Almost at the end of my circuit I didn't have enough copper tape so I got more and folded the ends so electricity could flow and that's how I fixed it.

The "other people" that Kevin referred to were the adult educators—he embraced the challenge of trying to figure it out himself.

As a multi-office collaborative team, we also had to do some reflecting and ask ourselves what worked, what needed to be modified, what needed to be eliminated or added, and where we went from there. Some things we learned:

Figure 8.16 Kevin proudly displays his copper tape circuit and LED light!

- Just because we knew about makerspaces did not mean that every teacher had this knowledge. We underestimated the learning curve for some of the teachers providing the makerspace pull-out program—the Maker Movement was still relatively new in K–12 education. We provided professional learning sessions and follow-up Google Hangouts, but we should have done the following:
  - *Spent more time focusing on nurturing the adult mindset.* Let them know that there will be struggle and that is expected.
  - *Frontloaded some of the information before the professional learning session.* There was way too much information in each day's training. Perhaps we could have sent a link to a video describing what a makerspace is so everyone would have some background knowledge when they walked in to the training. We could have also sent a link to the Google Classroom that was created for the teachers so they could have previewed the content.

- *Adjusted the timing.* We packed each student learning session full of ideas and guidance—too much of it! The sessions took longer than anticipated as students became engaged and wanted to explore further. We learned that the year 1 focus should remain only on circuits.
- Self-reflection is important, but I knew we also had to solicit feedback from the pull-out teachers as well. The teachers were invited to a meeting where I assured them that they would not hurt any feelings and encouraged them to be specific and honest about how the program had been implemented during the first year. This proved to be a valuable exercise that contributed to changes and improvements to the program.

Even though we recognized the changes we needed to make, year 1 of the program was overall a success. Students were excited to go to the makerspace, and they were engaged in the learning. Problem-solving skills got a great workout, as did reasoning and creativity. Perhaps most important is that these students learned about trial and error, perseverance, and productive struggle—lessons that they can transfer to other situations. Innovation occurs when we have the courage and comfort to make mistakes and learn from them; this applies to students as well as the adults who develop programs for them!

Facing Failure

Failure isn't an option is probably one of the worst phrases that exist (at least when it comes to growth mindset thinking). Failure is not only an option but is so very important on the path to learning and mastery of a skill. One of the areas where students struggle is with the idea of failure. This can be particularly hard for high-achieving students, perfectionists, and those students who live with strong parental pressure to succeed. Whenever possible, take opportunities to discuss the value of failure.

Asking students to analyze a scenario, quote, or movie clip can be an effective way to engage students in a discussion about the value of failure. For older students, analysis and interpretation of a quote such as Maya Angelou's "You may encounter many defeats, but you must not be defeated. In fact, it may be necessary to encounter the defeats, so you can know who you are, what you can rise from, how you can still come out of it" (1973) can serve as a vehicle to begin a critical discussion or debate about the value of failure.

Younger students can be shown a film clip and become engaged in discussion. As mentioned earlier, there is a scene in Disney's *Meet the Robinsons* movie where Lewis creates an invention that combines peanut butter and jelly and it fails (https://www.youtube .com/watch?v=V3UqEps1r5E). It is effective to stop the video clip right after Lewis buries his face in his hands and apologizes for the failure of his invention. Students can then be asked some of the following questions:

- How does the boy react to the way his invention worked?
- Why do you think he reacts this way?
- What do you think he will do next?
- If you were the boy, how would you react?
- How do you think the adults in the room will react to this situation? Why?

Continue to show the rest of the clip where the adults happily yell, "You've failed! From failure, you learn. From success…not so much." Continue engaging the students in a discussion:

- Why did the adults react this way?
- What does it mean when they say "From failure, you learn. From success…not so much"? Do you agree with this statement? Why or why not?
- Think of a time when you have failed at something. It might be schoolwork, learning to play a musical instrument, making a clay pot, ice skating…anything. (Give students an opportunity to think.) Now think about how you reacted to that failure. Did you give up? Try again in a different way? Try again the same way? Get angry? Cry? Celebrate?

- Let's brainstorm some ways that we can react in a positive way to failure. What are some things we can reflect on or ask ourselves when we do not succeed?

After this class discussion, continue to revisit the reflective aspect of reacting to failure throughout the year. This theme can be incorporated in writing assignments, debates, or analysis of characters, historical figures, and scientists who have failed. This learning experience can really make an impact with some students, who gain encouragement from seeing how effort and hard work can eventually pay off. In addition to discussion about the famous failures listed below, ask students to assume the point of view of the person involved in the failure. Some students may be willing to role-play. For example, give the students a scenario that is similar to the following: "You are a scientist whose job is to invent the strongest adhesive possible, but instead, you discover that you have developed a reusable adhesive. How would you react?" (This is actually how Post-it® notes were invented!)

Some examples of famous failures include:

- R. H. Macy: The founder of Macy's department store failed at seven previous business attempts.
- Colonel Sanders: Harland Davis Sanders's famous chicken was rejected 1,009 times before a restaurant accepted it.
- Thomas Edison: He conducted experiments on his concepts 9,000 times before he created the light bulb.
- Post-it® Notes: A scientist at 3M Company was working to create a super-strong adhesive; it was a failure. Instead, he accidentally made a reusable, pressure-sensitive adhesive that later was utilized in sticky notes.
- Chocolate Chip Cookies: Ruth Wakefield, owner of the Toll House Inn, was trying to make her chocolate cookie recipe and discovered that she was out of baker's chocolate. She decided to take sweet chocolate and break it into little pieces, adding them to the cookie dough and thinking that they would melt while they were baked. Instead, the

little pieces stayed together. She did not have her chocolate cookies in the end, but discovered the chocolate chip cookie through this failure!

A good book for middle and high school is *How They Choked: Failure, Flops, and Flaws of the Awfully Famous* (2016) by Georgia Bragg. This book highlights the mistakes of 14 well-known people, from Montezuma to Susan B. Anthony.

Analyzing Authors and Characters: A Sample Learning Task

With your students, brainstorm a list of characters that they have gotten to know through their reading during the year (elementary and middle school level) or brainstorm authors that they have studied (middle and high school level). Record the names on cards and group students in pairs or triads. Each group will be given a card with the name of a character or an author. (This is a great time to do some very subtle differentiation by giving more complex character or author cards to students who embrace challenge.) Each group will analyze the character or author's actions/words/written word through a growth or fixed mindset lens. For example, some second-grade characters might include Grace, from *Amazing Grace*, Iggy Peck, from *Iggy Peck, Architect*, or Ada Twist, from *Ada Twist, Scientist*.

An example of an author list for a 10th-grade English course might include Henry Thoreau, Ralph Waldo Emerson, Emily Dickinson, Frederick Douglass, F. Scott Fitzgerald, and Mark Twain. Teachers can write options for authors to study on index cards and hand them out. In pairs or triads, students should discuss what they know about each author and look for additional information as needed. Students will be asked to find evidence in the author's life or his or her writings that may suggest a fixed and/or growth mindset mentality. They must be prepared to justify their decision with specific evidence. For example, a group of students might share:

We think that Frederick Douglass has a growth mindset for many reasons. A specific example of how he valued effort and perseverance can be found on page 58 of *Narrative of the Life of Frederick Douglass*, where he explains the process of how he learned to read and write in a very non-traditional manner by copying letters that were marked on timber as well as other innovative ways. He states, "Thus after a long, tedious effort for years, I finally succeeded in learning how to write." Other examples of a growth mindset in Frederick Douglass's life include...

After each group states its argument, cards should be classified into three possible groups: Fixed Mindset, Growth Mindset, and Both Fixed and Growth Mindset. Students can then look at the categories and perhaps begin to make some generalizations about authors, time periods, literary philosophies, and movements in relation to a growth or fixed mindset.

A similar task can incorporate video clips of real-life or movie characters into the classroom. Have students discuss what they see in the film clips and analyze and classify the characters' reactions using a chart similar to the one created for the author studies.

Concept Placemats

The concept placement strategy was inspired by the concept formation model. It is similar to a collection, only it typically builds a more abstract concept and uses only one piece of paper or smart-board display. A concept placemat can be developed easily using a computer and clip art; the more challenging part is deciding what images will be used to communicate the concept.

Concept formation relates to making connections, seeing relationships between items of information, and defining a concept from them. Concept formation is a key skill required for learning new ideas. Is there a concept based on a content area that is being studied that you would like your students to form using images? Choosing a more abstract concept works best. For example, "relationships" works better than "pets." Some other guidelines for developing concept placemats include:

- Once you choose a concept, brainstorm ideas about what kinds of images might represent that particular concept. (Three to six images are usually enough to build a concept.)
- In the middle of the concept placemat, place a text box that says, "Find pairs of objects that share a common concept. Find three objects that share a common concept. What concept do all of these images have in common? Be prepared to justify your thinking."

Next, within an instructional sequence, determine how the placemat will be used: As a preassessment or formative assessment? Activator? As a vehicle for learning new information? As a springboard for a discussion? The possibilities are endless.

Ask students to look at the placemat quietly. Give everyone a set time (1–2 minutes), then ask for ideas (otherwise the "dominators" rule) using questions similar to these:

- Who can find two things that share a common concept or are the same in some way? (Take all student responses. During this time, observe/listen for unique connections between the images.)
- Who can find three things that share a common concept or are the same in some way? (Take all student responses. During this time, observe/listen for unique connections between the images.)
- Now, let's look for some things that share a common concept or are the same among all of the images. (Take all student responses. During this time, observe/listen for unique connections between the images—ask for them to justify their thinking if needed.)

- Let's hear some ideas for adding more things that also share the same concept.
- Let's think about why I might have chosen this concept for our class. What do you think we will be talking about? What do you think we are going to learn about? (This question should ask about the content connection of the strategy.)

Concept placemats you may consider developing include the following:

- *Concept Placemat #1: Things That Have Potential.* Images can include: flowers being watered, a solar panel, blueprints for a building, a child with blocks, a young child flexing his muscles, and for older students, a pineapple. The pineapple demonstrates potential because it is often harvested before it is fully grown so that the size is consistent when it is cored, sliced, and fitted into its can. An additional discussion can occur about the potential the pineapple may have if it were allowed to continue growing. Would it be sweeter? Juicier? How large would it grow? Relate the concept placemat and discussion back to the students' own potential. (See Figure 8.17.)
- *Concept Placemat #2: Neural Networks: Study Habits That Help the Brain Learn.* Images can include: two students working together (collaborative learning), a mnemonic device such as HOMES for the Great Lakes, a picture of various types of flashcards, a mathematical formula being repeated (repetition), and a child thinking about new learning and applying it to other things. After the discussion of the concept, students can use this to reflect on their own study habits and make plans for improving these habits. (See Figure 8.18.)
- *Concept Placemat #3: Attention and Concentration: Things That Help the Brain Focus.* Images can include: a plate with foods that represent a good breakfast, an image that represents

Find pairs of objects that share a common concept.
Find three objects that share a common concept.

What concept do all of these images have in common?
Be prepared to tell why.

Figure 8.17 Concept placemat example

Figure 8.18 Concept placemat example

no TV or electronics, a child sleeping, children playing a sport outside, a student using all of his or her senses: hearing, seeing, smelling, tasting, and touching. Discussion can focus on why these things can help the brain work to the best of its ability. Students can make a plan for improving their own brain function. (See Figure 8.19.)

Teaching Optimism

Can optimism be taught? Let's think about the opposite of optimism—pessimism. Many of us have what I refer to as an Eeyore in their life. Remember Eeyore, the donkey from Winnie the Pooh? Eeyore just shuffled along and saw things through a pessimistic lens. Some of us might live with an Eeyore, some of us work with an Eeyore, and some of us are friends with an Eeyore. What happens if we spend too much time with an Eeyore? We can pick up on the same behaviors! Pessimism is contagious—did you ever sit at a meeting or professional learning session and someone at the table starts complaining, "She doesn't know what she is talking about," "That will never work here," or "Here comes a new initiative that will disappear in a few months"? On many occasions, others at the table begin adopting the same pessimistic mindset. The good news is that optimism can be just as contagious as pessimism!

An optimistic brain is a happy brain. Neuroscientists have discovered that consistent negative or positive thoughts and feelings can affect brain activity and have an impact on learning. The good news is that you can train your brain to help you become a more optimistic person. It just makes sense that a growth mindset classroom is an optimistic classroom. Some relatively simple routines can be put in place in a classroom that will nurture optimism.

The first is a gratitude journal. Students should be given opportunities several times a week to write in their gratitude journal. They can simply write a list of things they are grateful for or write a paragraph or two about a specific event that they are grateful for. A kindergarten classroom that I was visiting volunteered to share their journals with me. They were to write or draw the things they

Figure 8.19 Concept placemat example

were grateful for. I saw lots of pictures of toys, video consoles, food, and family. I noticed that one young boy drew a picture of a watch. When I asked him why he was grateful for a watch, he explained that it was actually his father's watch that had been given to him by his father (the young boy's grandfather). He had found out recently that this watch would someday be his, and he realized that this was a very special watch. Thus, he showed gratitude for something that would happen in his future.

One Christmas, my 15-year-old daughter decided to give all of her friends a gratitude jar. She decorated each jar and wrote a message asking her friends to take a small piece of paper (which she supplied) and on each day of the coming year, write one thing they were grateful for. Then on New Year's Eve they would all get together and count their many blessings from the previous year. Teachers can put a similar process in place in their classrooms. Each day every student can respond to a prompt, like "Something good that happened to me today," "A reason that I have a great life," or "I am grateful for these things today." Students would drop the responses into a personal or communal box. What this exercise does is practice optimism. By asking students to look at the good in every day, they are training their brains to be optimistic. Of course, optimism must be modeled and practiced by the teachers and school staff each day.

Growth Mindset Reminders in the Classroom

In addition to presenting specific lessons about the malleability of the mind and using online resources, think of ways that the message can be embedded within the content of instruction and the learning atmosphere of the classroom. The following are some visual triggers that can be posted in the classroom or in the school hallways that can be used to reinforce the message:

- Growth Mindset Poster (see Figure 8.14)
- Picture of a neuron or plushy neurons (perhaps with names like Ned and Nellie Neuron?)

- Pictures of people who exemplify a growth mindset:
  - Elementary classrooms: Michael Jordan, Oprah Winfrey, Abraham Lincoln, Nelson Mandela, Beethoven, Babe Ruth, Frederick Douglass
  - STEM Classrooms: Mae Jemison, Ada Lovelace, Albert Einstein, Robert Goddard, Bill Gates, Katherine Johnson, Leland Melvin
  - English/Reading Classrooms: Emily Dickinson, Langston Hughes, Agatha Christie, Stephen King
- Inspirational quotes that contribute to a growth mindset:
  - "We keep moving forward, opening new doors, and doing new things, because we're curious and curiosity keeps leading us down new paths" (Walt Disney)
  - "You may encounter many defeats, but you must not be defeated. In fact, it may be necessary to encounter the defeats, so you can know who you are, what you can rise from, how you can still come out of it" (Maya Angelou)
  - "All of old. Nothing else ever. Ever tried. Ever failed. No matter. Try again. Fail again. Fail better" (Samuel Beckett)
  - "Instead of letting your hardships and failures discourage or exhaust you, let them inspire you. Let them make you even hungrier to succeed" (Michelle Obama)
  - "It does not matter how slowly you go as long as you do not stop" (Confucius)
  - "It always seems impossible until it's done" (Nelson Mandela)
  - "Never confuse a single defeat with a final defeat" (F. Scott Fitzgerald)
  - "Once you learn to quit, it becomes a habit" (Vince Lombardi Jr.)

Student Goal-Setting

Students of all ages should engage in setting and working toward learning goals. A great place to start is setting growth mindset goals. Once students begin learning some of the tenets of a growth mindset, they can begin setting individual growth mindset goals. Whether they are growth mindset goals or academic goals, they should always be process goals not product goals. Instead of saying, "My goal is to get an A in English," the goal might be "My goal is to read text selections as soon as they are assigned and reread sections that I don't understand." Growth mindset goals can be less content-specific; the following examples of more generic mindset goals are adapted from *Ready-to-Use Resources for Mindsets in the Classroom* (Ricci, 2020):

- I will review all of my work that is returned and modify or redo it to improve it.
- I will use a variety of strategies (look at past work, review notes, use online resources) when I get stuck on something.
- I will request time after class to work with my teacher if I don't understand a concept yet.
- I will ask for more challenging work if the work presented does not require much effort.

Take a look at Catherine's growth mindset goal in Figure 8.20. She finds herself thinking "I can't do this" as soon as she experiences the slightest bit of struggle, and she wants to work on changing that.

Focus on the Specific Actions of Growth-Oriented People

Learning about people who exemplified a growth mindset throughout their life can be a powerful catalyst for students. I had the privilege of speaking with astronaut Leland Melvin at an event where we were both keynote speakers. (These were well-thought-out keynotes from the conference planners—learning about mindsets and then hearing about how growth mindset thinking comes to fruition through a personal story.) As he spoke about his life, I couldn't help but think about the resilience, perseverance, and grit that he demonstrated. Before we ever heard of the term makerspace, Leland grew up in one. He shared a story about how his

My Growth Mindset Goal

Name: Catherine   Date: September 7

Growth Mindset Goal: I will not think or say, "I can't do this."

I hope to reach my goal by: September 18

Strategies or things I might do to help reach my goal:
When work is hard for me I will visualize neurons trying to connect in my brain. When I start to think that I can't do it, I will try to persevere until it starts making sense. I will ask for help if these don't work.

Check-in: How am I doing toward this Growth Mindset Goal? Date: September 14

☐ I have met this goal   ☐ I have partially met this goal   ☑ I have not met this goal yet

An example of something I did that made me realize that I have met, have partially met, or have not yet met this goal:
My mind automatically goes to "I can't do this" whenever I feel challenged. I don't want to make mistakes so I give up.

Some new strategies to try or my new growth mindset goal:
Every time that happens I will talk myself out of a fixed mindset and talk my way into a growth mindset. I will remind myself that making mistakes is part of learning something new. I will put a small picture of a neuron on the corner of my desk to remind myself that my brain is getting stronger when I think hard. I will adjust my target date to September 30.

(If you have a new goal, get a blank Growth Mindset Goal form.)

Figure 8.20 Sample growth mindset goal

father purchased an old bread delivery truck and the whole family worked together tirelessly one summer to repurpose it into a recreational vehicle (RV) with beds, electricity, and plumbing! Talk about project-based learning!

Leland also had obstacles in his life: He was a star football player in college and was drafted by the Detroit Lions, but suffered an injury so they released him. He was then picked up by the Dallas Cowboys and had another injury that ended his football career. His career as an astronaut was also sidelined due to hearing loss from an ear injury that he suffered during a training exercise, but he eventually went to space despite his setback. Through the many ups and downs in Leland's life, he persevered.

Students can research people who demonstrated a fixed or growth mindset thinking. Emphasis in their research could be focused on how those important noncognitive skills affected their lives. What if Leland had given up his job at NASA after he lost some of his hearing? How might his life have been different?

Another possibility is Simon Rodia, an Italian immigrant who created the amazing Watts Towers sculptures in California. He persevered for 30 years, creating beautiful mosaics out of broken dishware and ceramics. The picture book, *Dream Something Big: The Story of the Watts Towers* (Aston, 2011), tells the story of Rodia and can be used with kids of all ages as a way to discuss perseverance and motivation. What was his motivation as he toiled for years creating the Watts Towers?

Many ways exist to continue building the growth mindset message in the classroom. The most important element is being consistent with the message. The next chapter offers some ways to maintain a growth mindset culture.

References

Angelou, M. (1973, November 21). You may encounter many defeats, but you must not be defeated. In fact, it may be necessary to encounter the defeats, so you can know who you are, what you can rise from, how you can still come out of it. Interview with

Bill Moyer A Conversation with Maya Angelou. Retrieved from https://billmoyers.com/content/conversation-maya-angelou/.

Bruner, J. S. (1961). The act of discovery. *Harvard Educational Review, 31,* 21–32.

Douglass, F. 1818–1895. (2003). *Narrative of the life of Frederick Douglass, an American slave.* Boston, MA: Bedford/St. Martin's.

Harrigan, W., & Commons, M. (2014). The stage of development of a species predicts the number of neurons. *Behavioral Development Bulletin, 19*(4), 12–21.

Ricci, M. C. (2018). *Create a Growth Mindset School: An administrators guide to leading a growth mindset community.* Waco, TX: Prufrock Press.

Ricci, M. C. (2018). *Nothing you can't do! The secret power of a growth mindset.* Waco, TX: Prufrock Press.

Ricci, M. C. (2020). *Ready to use resources for mindsets in the classroom: Everything educators need for building growth mindset learning communities.* Prufrock Press.

Ricci, M. C., & Lee, M. (2024). *Mindsets for parents: Strategies to encourage growth mindsets in kids.* Waco, TX: Prufrock Press.

CHAPTER 9

WHAT ARE SOME WAYS SCHOOL STAFF CAN MAINTAIN A GROWTH MINDSET SCHOOL CULTURE?

"I think my head is going to explode from all the neurons connecting in my head!"
—Grade 2 student

The importance of continually reinforcing the growth mindset message every day cannot be emphasized enough. Maintaining perseverance and effort is a challenge for some students, and they need to be continually reminded that they can achieve success. Specific plans to maintain a growth mindset school culture should be embedded in yearly school improvement plans to ensure that they are monitored. During each staff meeting, at least 15 minutes should be dedicated to discussion about maintaining your school's growth mindset culture. Identify areas of strength and areas that could use improvement.

One aspect of a growth mindset school that is often overlooked is the learning environment in the classrooms. A growth mindset classroom must be a safe place where students do not feel judged and are free to take intellectual risks. A trusting, positive relationship between teacher and student is the heart of a secure learning environment.

The learning environment should also be a fear-free zone. Fear is such an intense emotion that it can shut down cognitive processes and force the brain to only focus on the source of the fear and what to do about it. The fear of making an error or experiencing failure is a big obstacle to learning. As mentioned earlier, some students will avoid experiences that may be too challenging due to fear of failure. A teacher who embraces growth mindset thinking should discuss these fears with students and reassure them that they will not be judged if they make mistakes or fail. Teachers can also share their own stories of times that they were afraid to take a risk due to fear. Our environment helps to shape us, and a classroom learning environment does as well: "Just as adults are affected by their environments, students are encouraged or discouraged, energized or deflated, invited or alienated by classroom environments" (Sousa & Tomlinson, 2011, p. 31). Also important to note is that it can pose a challenge for students to feel supported in a learning environment where work is either too hard or too easy for them; thus, a differentiated, responsive classroom contributes to an intellectually safe learning environment.

Also be aware of physical things in your learning environment that might be sending fixed mindset messages. Bulletin boards and displays should not be an array of "A" or perfect papers. Student work should be displayed, but think carefully about the message they send. For example, you could post your students' first draft or first attempt at something and right next to it display a later attempt to highlight the growth that students make. You can also display things that highlight the different strategies that students use to learn—perhaps examples of how two or three different students approached the same math problem in different ways. What about the names of those displays? Titles like "Top Dogs!" and one I saw not too long ago, "Hanging Out With Perfect Papers!" can send fixed mindset messages to kids. Instead, try titles like "Look How We Grow" or "All-Star Effort."

Look at the stickers or words that you write on students' papers, too. Do they say things like "Superstar!" or "Brilliant!"? Instead, try growth mindset messages like "Great Effort!", "You're showing a lot of progress!", or "You don't quite understand YET." Take a look around your room: Is there anything else that might inadvertently sabotage your growth mindset space?

Think about events you have in your school, such as awards programs and honor roll assemblies. They may elicit accolades for those children who reach a specific level of performance, but consider that some "winners" put forth little effort to reach the mark and others put forth tremendous effort and miss it by an inch. An educator in Colorado explained that in her school they hold honor roll assemblies quarterly, and the same kids were always sitting in the back two rows—those who were never recognized. She shared that these assemblies took place for two reasons: to motivate students who are not recognized (I don't think that is working because the same students always remain seated) and because it is a tradition in the school that the parents expect (We need to look carefully at some of our school traditions through a mindset lens). What is the point of an honor roll assembly? If the response is to recognize good grades, I would argue that the "reward" could be the grade—if the student actually worked for it. Some students receive A's without putting forth a whole lot of effort (these students are likely underchallenged). If the response is to motivate others, then, take note: are the same students being unrecognized every time? Does an honor roll assembly really motivate others? An event such as this should shift its purpose to celebrate growth and hard work rather than grades.

At Thurmont Primary School in Thurmont, MD, students participate in a Growth Parade twice a year—at the halfway point as well as at the end of the school year. Each child creates a sign that proclaims something that they have grown in, and they (and their teachers) proudly march through the school holding up their signs. Some of the signs said the following:

- I made it to Level 7 in Lexia!
- I got better at telling time to the nearest minute!
- I got better at art (and he drew Spider-Man on the sign to prove it!).

179

Coaching

Instructional coaching positions have been added to many schools and districts across the country. This "coach" provides non-evaluative feedback about instruction to teachers—coaches observe, model, plan, and can team with teachers to bring best instructional practices into classrooms. I would argue that the most important part of the coach's role is to establish a trusting partnership with the coachee. Instructional coaches must have a growth mindset about the people with whom they work. They must believe that with guidance, strategies, and modelling from the coach, coupled with motivation and effort from the teacher, instruction can grow and improve.

Equally important is the mindset of the coachee. Many educators welcome coaches into their classrooms—they want feedback and they want to improve their skills. Many value the coach-teacher relationship—it is a space where they can ask questions and try new strategies without the fear of being evaluated (the coach should never act as an informant to the school administration). Coaching can also focus on growth mindset learning in the classroom—feedback can be targeted to delivery of feedback and praise toward students, responsive, differentiated opportunities for all students, critical thinking strategies, goal-setting lessons, etc.

There are a few educators who may not welcome coaches into their classroom; this happens for a multitude of reasons, one being that teachers don't feel that they need coaching (everything is going great, their students achieve, they are confident teachers who do not see the need for feedback). Studies suggest that some overconfident people tend to apply fixed mindset thinking. If you think about it, it makes sense: they might think, "I don't need to learn anything new because I am already good at it." Another reason why teachers may not like to work with coaches is due to lack of confidence or fear of judgment; this is why trust is so important between the coach and teacher.

Coaching serves as an effective way to improve teaching and learning in the classroom. When both coach and teacher apply growth mindset thinking, it is a wonderful collaboration!

A Growth Mindset School

Within the context of instruction, the growth mindset message can also be reinforced. For example, the staff at Maryvale Elementary School in Rockville, MD, was very committed to building a growth mindset school culture. The school's principal, Karen Gregory, presented each staff member with a growth mindset T-shirt (see Figure 9.1) during preservice week. Over a two-year period, the staff participated in ongoing professional learning sessions about ways to build and maintain this school culture.

On one visit to Maryvale, teachers were asked to look carefully at their curriculum and identify places where they could embed the growth mindset message. This exercise allowed the staff to take ownership of the message—they looked at curriculum in a new way, through the lens of opportunities to nurture resiliency, effort, intellectual risk-taking, and perseverance. Figure 9.2 shows an example of how the staff looked at their current curricula and thought about ways the concept of growth mindset could be incorporated.

Figure 9.1 Karen Gregory (center) and some of her Maryvale staff members in their growth mindset T-shirts

Content Area	Unit, Book, Resource, Topic	Growth or Fixed Mindset Example	Comments, Additional Information
Reading	*Lily and Miss Liberty* By Carla Stevens	Lily demonstrates persistence/effort	Historical Fiction Grade 3
Social Studies	Wampanoag Culture	Analyze the Wampanoag for evidence of a growth or fixed mindset	Grade 2
English	*Good Night, Mr. Tom* By Michelle Magorian	Analysis of characters through the lens of a growth mindset	Middle School Historical Fiction WWII
Reading	*Wilma Unlimited: How Wilma Rudolph Became the World's Fastest Woman* By Kathleen Krull	Find evidence in Wilma's life that demonstrates perseverance, motivation, and effort.	Grades K–3 Biography
History	Susan B. Anthony was a women's rights activist who spent her entire life working for a constitutional amendment giving women the right to vote.	Susan B. Anthony overcame obstacles and persisted in the face of setbacks.	High School American History

Figure 9.2 Incorporating mindsets into the content areas in one school

Schools could brainstorm "Look Fors" that would demonstrate a growth mindset school and class culture, including evidence of a differentiated, responsive classroom. These are practices that should be evident in a classroom's physical and affective environment as well as observed through teacher-student interaction. "Look Fors" for a differentiated, responsive, growth mindset classroom might look like the list in Figure 9.3.

To work toward a growth mindset school culture is a commitment that all stakeholders must make. Be cognizant of new educators joining your staff and have a plan for getting them on board with your growth mindset goals. Continually monitor and reflect on practices that are having an impact and those that need to be improved upon. Would visitors to your school pick up on the persistence and effort that your students are putting forth? Are more students embracing challenging tasks? Are teachers using language that acknowledges what students do rather than who they are? Are students using growth mindset language and talking about neural connections? Are expectations high for all students?

Look Fors in a Differentiated, Responsive Classroom

Ongoing Assessment
- Preassessment with previewing and analysis is consistently used.
- Alternative challenging opportunities and instruction are provided when proficiency is demonstrated.
- Teachers use formative assessments regularly to find students who are ready for more challenge.
- Opportunities for students to self-assess are used routinely.
- Incorrect answers are circled so students know to look at them again—redos and retakes are part of the culture in the classroom.

Flexible/Fluid Grouping Practices
- Flexible subgrouping is an integral part of programming.
- Anchor activities and/or meaningful centers are used to facilitate management of groups.

Figure 9.3 Sample list of "Look Fors"

Curriculum Compacting
- Teachers enable some students to eliminate and/or take less time to learn material.

Expectations
- Teacher expectations are high for all students.
- Students and teachers believe in the ability to develop intelligence.
- Recognition of intellectual potential is not entirely dependent on performance in reading/writing/math. Potential is also recognized through discussion, questions, and responses.
- Teacher provides many opportunities for students to think for themselves.

Questioning
- Students are given many opportunities to respond to and ask higher level questions.

Higher Level Thinking
- Instructional strategies that nurture/promote higher level thinking are embedded in everyday instruction (concept attainment/formation, interpretation, reasoning, problem solving, evaluating).

Acceleration and Enrichment
- Individuals or groups of students are given opportunities to excel beyond grade-level expectations across content areas.
- Opportunities for enrichment occur through application of and reasoning with content, guest speakers, mentors, and technology.
- Teacher supplements or modifies curriculum to facilitate high-level learning.
- Instruction consists of advanced content and differentiated strategies to reflect the intellectual processes of high-potential learners.
- Above-grade-level materials are available to students across content areas.
- Students are given opportunities for in-depth study/research.

Classroom Environment
- Intellectual risk-taking is evident.
- A growth mindset class culture exists.
- Learning stations and/or anchor activities are evident in classroom.
- Room arrangement is conducive to group work.
- A variety of student work samples are displayed.
- A wealth of resources at many levels are available to students.

Beware of the False Growth Mindset!

Carol Dweck (2015) and her colleagues have defined a "false growth mindset" as that demonstrated in a person who says that he or she has a growth mindset, but whose actions say otherwise. We all need to be very aware of some of the things that we might do in the name of "growth mindset" but are actually quite the opposite—fixed mindset actions. One of the reasons that this is occurring is because adults are not giving themselves the time to really examine their own mindsets. A mindset does not change after one faculty meeting or watching one TED talk. It is a journey. It takes time and practice to transition learning environments. One especially challenging transition is the belief that process is just as (and sometimes more) important than the outcome.

An example of a false growth mindset is when we are hyperfocused on grades and test scores, which can stand in the way of a growth mindset. We may communicate growth mindset messages all day to our students, then spend time speaking to students about grades—"You should have worked harder"—rather than discussing the process of studying and learning the material. We may not build in time to reteach or clarify concepts—these are fixed mindset actions. Dweck also cautioned that it is a disservice to say things like, "You can do anything that you put your mind to." Yes, it is an important message, but when it is said, it is important to consider if the student has the experience and knowledge to make it happen. Dweck explained it like this: "While this may be true, simply asserting it does not make it so, particularly when students don't yet have the knowledge, skills, strategies, or resources to bring this about" (para. 8).

Leadership

Before I leave you, let's give a little attention to leadership in schools; (present leaders as well as those aspiring to be in a leadership position) this includes, but is not limited to, grade level team leaders, department chairs, special education leaders, instructional coaches, data coaches, and of course assistant principals and principals. The first step in leading your team toward a growth mindset school is self-reflection.

Respond to the following questions—yes, they are yes or no questions, but explain why you answered the way you did.

- Do you embrace growth and continuous improvement?
- Are you coachable?
- Do you learn and make changes based on the feedback of others? Why?
- Are you inspired by others' success rather than feeling threatened or envious?
- Do you compete against yourself, not others?
- Are you comfortable with not being perfect and making errors?
- Do you project enthusiasm and positive energy?

Take a look at the Growth Mindset Attributes Leadership Reflection (Figure 9.4). These are some of the attributes that growth mindset leaders demonstrate. Think about where you are on the scale in relation to your role as a leader.

Choose one or two areas where you would like to improve and grow and make a list of some doable actions that will help you grow in that area. For example, if you chose Optimism, you may spend a few minutes each morning saying affirmations:

- I will assume positive intentions from my team.
- Today will be a great day.
- I am growing every day.
- I have the support that I need.

If you are speaking to a team member or student about an incident, you may practice taking a minute and thinking about the intention of the incident before speaking or making a decision. You have probably already thought about the fact that these attributes are not just for school leaders; they can help all of us become better at what we do.

Growth Mindset Attributes Leadership Reflection

The following are some of the attributes that growth mindset leaders demonstrate. Think about where you are on each scale in relation to your role as a leader.

1 – Not at all   5 – Always

		OPTIMISTIC		
1	2	3	4	5

		SUPPORTIVE		
1	2	3	4	5

		OPEN-MINDED		
1	2	3	4	5

		INQUISITIVE		
1	2	3	4	5

		RESILIENT		
1	2	3	4	5

		FLEXIBLE		
1	2	3	4	5

		TRUSTWORTHY		
1	2	3	4	5

		A FOCUSED LISTENER		
1	2	3	4	5

		A RISK TAKER		
1	2	3	4	5

Figure 9.4 Growth Mindset Atttributes Leadership Reflection

References

Dweck, C. (2015). Carol Dweck revisits the growth mindset. *Education Week.* Retrieved from http://www.edweek.org/ew/articles/2015/09/23/carol-dweck-revisits-the-growth-mindset.html.

Sousa, D. A., & Tomlinson, C. A. (2011). *Differentiation and the brain: How neuroscience supports the learner-friendly classroom.* Bloomington, IN: Solution Tree Press.

CHAPTER 10

SUMMARY

"If you don't practice, your neural connection will break!"–Grade 2 student

The commitment to building and maintaining a learning environment where expectations are high for all students, responsive instruction is the norm, and where all students value effort and perseverance is well worth the time. Adopting some of the components will incite some change, but in order to have the most impact, a symphony of the following should occur:

- Educators who believe that all students can achieve and be successful.
- Students who have a conceptual understanding of neural connections and believe that with effort and perseverance they can learn, be successful, and grow their intelligence.
- Differentiated, responsive instruction that meets students where they are, giving them what they need, when they need it, and how they need it.
- Critical thinking opportunities that are embedded in curriculum, instruction, and assessment.
- A broadened conception of "Giftedness" that is focused on talent development and domain-specific strength, and relies heavily on the word "potential" rather than the word "Gifted."

Educators teach students, not curriculum. It is time to meet students where they are, expect the best from all of them, and provide opportunities for each and every student to succeed. A growth mindset school culture will most definitely open doors for all students.

On a personal note, many years ago I was deep into the whole malleable intelligence, growth, and fixed mindset research and provided many professional development sessions to teachers, parents, and administrators on the topic. It was after one of these sessions that I was approached by a participant who suggested that I write a book about the educational implications of growth and fixed mindsets. She shared that she thought I had a lot to offer educators and had the potential to have a positive impact on children. I thanked her for the nice compliment and, well, I hate to admit it, but a fixed mindset mentality sprang right back into my head and I thought, "I could never write a book." About a month later, I heard Carol Dweck speak at the National Association for Gifted Children conference, and on the plane ride home, I began the first edition of this book. The process was not easy. Yes, there were times when I considered giving up, but I persevered. As I wrote the last few lines, I noticed that the laundry needed to be done, I had to prepare for a presentation for the next day, the dog had to be taken out, and my daughter was asking for homework help. Juggling family, a new job, and writing was one of the greatest challenges of my life, but I did it…with lots of hard work and effort.

During the second update in 2018, a different set of challenges presented itself. I had planned on finishing the update for this book during the six weeks that I would be on leave from my "real job" recovering from knee replacement surgery. Prior to the surgery, I gathered my research, created a space that held all of my notes and references, placed it next to my recliner where I knew I would be elevating my new knee—I was ready! Ha! Even though I read, joined online support groups, and followed blogs dealing with recovery, I was not prepared for what I experienced. What I experienced were slow, painful, sleep-deprived, brain-fogged early weeks of recovery. I thought for sure each day would be better—not so in the early weeks…or at least it didn't feel that way. One of the recovery blogs I was on had daily inspirational messages to encourage those in the early weeks of recovery, and I found myself mumbling under my breath when I read things like "Pain is temporary and victory is forever" or "Be positive, patient, and persistent." Those darn quotes just made me mad—I didn't want to be patient. I just wanted to feel better and be able to move! When I was ten weeks post-surgery, with a clearer head, I tried to analyze why I morphed into that fixed mindset mentality. I know the benefits of a growth mindset and I was stuck for weeks fighting fixed mindset thinking. I realize it probably had something to do with the combination of pain and inactivity. The experience taught me a few things about mindsets—sometimes the barriers are strong and frustration can get the best of us, but these are the times that resilience and perseverance are even more important. (This time around, for the third edition, my biggest obstacle was a puppy who has taken over the house!)

If you are interested in doing an in-person or virtual book club with this book, *Ready to Use Resources for Mindsets in the Classroom* includes a chapter with a variety of book club models that have been used across the country. You can contact me via my website www.marycayricci.com about scheduling a free virtual visit to one of your sessions.

If you would like to share any of your growth mindset school experiences or have a question for me, please always feel free to reach out to me through my website or through social media Twitter (X) or Threads (@marycayr). I have seen so many positive outcomes for students and educators; I can't wait for you to see them as well!

On the following pages, you will find a list of videos, songs, and books that you can use to supplement the growth mindset learning experiences for your learners.

Remember that building a growth mindset learning environment is a journey—a journey for you as an educator reflecting on your own mindset as well as your students. You will get there—with dedication, hard work, and a growth mindset.

APPENDIX A

WEBSITES, VIDEOS, AND BOOKS

Websites

- **Neuroscience for Kids** http://faculty.washington.edu/chudler/neurok.html

  This site includes lesson plans, science fair projects, and memory and learning games. It also has some great brain songs for our young learners ("I've Been Working on the Neurons" and "Home on the Brain"), synaptic tag, and other outdoor brain games.
- **How Stuff Works** http://science.howstuffworks.com/life/inside-the-mind/human-brain/brain.htm

  This site's explanation of the brain and how it works is good for middle school and high school students.

- **BrainFacts** http://www.brainfacts.org

This site explains neuroscience core concepts and includes lots of resources for teachers.

Videos and Songs

- *How To Grow Your Brain* (4 minutes) https://www.youtube.com/watch?v=GWSZ1DKjNzY&sns=fb

This Khan Academy video discusses the ways our brain is like a muscle—it requires exercise.

- *Learning—How it Works & How to Do it Better* (11:39 minutes) https://www.youtube.com/watch?v=u9WpHHJz5Dc

A Trevor Ragan video that highlights that we learn to do things and that we are not born with knowledge, strengths, and weaknesses. This message is backed up by basic understanding of the brain. We are not "prewired" to do things well—as he puts it, the Babies and Butt-kickers learn like "maniacs" (Grades 5–adult).

- *Growth Mindset Animation* (3:50 minutes) https://www.youtube.com/watch?v=-_oqghnxBmY&sns=fb

This is a basic introduction to growth and fixed mindsets.

- *Gregor Townsend–Coaching and Growth Mindset* (5:58 minutes) https://www.youtube.com/watch?v=t4-3Zb6cyes&feature=youtu.be

Gregor Townsend, Coach of Glasgow Warriors (Scotland), explains how he uses a growth mindset with the rugby players he coaches.

- *Stuck on an Escalator* (2 minutes) https://www.youtube.com/watch?v=Kq65aAYCHOw

A great video to view prior to a discussion of the importance of using strategies when you are stuck on something.

- *Perseverance. The Story of Nick Vujicic* (3.5 minutes) https://www.youtube.com/watch?v=gNnVdlvodTQ

This video focuses on the life of Nick Vujicic, a man born with no arms or legs, but who demonstrates a growth mindset.

- *Shakira–Try Everything* (3 minutes) https://www.youtube.com/watch?v=c6rP-YP4c5I

This is the song and video for "Try Everything," a growth mindset song, from the movie *Zootopia*.

- *Growth Mindset for Students–Episode 1/5* (2 minutes) https://www.youtube.com/watch?v=2zrtHt3bBmQ

Mojo the friendly monster doesn't think he is smart enough for school until his friend Katie explains to him that his brain is like a muscle and everyone can get smarter, in this video by ClassDojo.

- *The Incredible Power of Yet* (2:35 minutes) https://www.youtube.com/watch?v=i8AN9tu9Y84

- *Perseverance for Students–Episode 1/3* (4:19 minutes) https://www.youtube.com/watch?v=IOaFwwLyTRo &t=88s

Katie is worried about the art show until she reads about Thomas Edison. She has an imaginary conversation with Edison about the learning "dip" in this video by ClassDojo.

- *Sesame Street: Bruno Mars: Don't Give Up* (2 minutes) https://www.youtube.com/watch?v=pWp6kkz-pnQ

Bruno Mars and his Muppet friends sing about the importance of not giving up.

- *Sesame Street: Janelle Monae– The Power of Yet* (2:41 minutes) https://www.youtube.com/watch?v=XLeUvZvuvAs

Janelle Monae sings to her Muppet friends about working hard, staying focused, and eventually getting to where you want to be. That's the "Power of Yet." (I was in a school where all the kindergarten kids were singing this through the halls!)

- *Elmo Doesn't Give Up Song (Yet Song): Sesame Street: Little Children, Big Challenges* (2 minutes) https://www.youtube.com/watch?v=vchWYQyZtec&list=PLQxsdrYsW5QsVIu39pVwIJui-XcR1Pq1l&index=5

Elmo and a friend sing about how even though Elmo might not be able to do some things right now, he should keep trying.

- *Soar: 3-D Animated Short by Alyce Tzue* (5 minutes) https://www.youtube.com/watch?v=UUIaseGrkLc&list=PLz9udltW-0Sp0vtuP5AWOiLSa6nprxOoE

This 3-D animated short called "Soar" (with no dialogue) is about a young girl who must help a tiny pilot fly because she has a very important task to complete perseverance and a variety of strategies help!

- *The Power of Yet-Trevor Muir* (2.5 minutes) https://www.youtube.com/watch?v=NcaoWeVOKls

Inspirational message about getting better at anything you want to. Good for middle and high school students.

- *I Can't Do That Yet! Book Read-Aloud* (11 min) https://www.youtube.com/watch?v=fwLiUCWCUrU

Can't Do That...YET! Is a read where the main character, Enna doesn't have much self-confidence. She's worried that she can't do things on her own. She comes to realize that she can do great things...just not *yet*!

- *C.J Luckey The Power of Yet* (3.5 min) https://www.youtube.com/watch?v=J6CnrFvY94E

The official music video for The Power of Yet—from C.J. Lucky's album, C.A.P.S. (**C**elebrating **A**ll **P**ersevering **S**tudents)

- *"The Power of Yet" with Gromo & friends* (3.4 min) https://www.youtube.com/watch?v=Mjw0EpPHLlE

Frankie discovers the power of yet. Through careful coaching from Gromo, she shifts her mindset away from the idea that we are either good or not good at something, towards the concept of yet and the need for courage in developing abilities.

- *Mineola Grows: A Learner's Guide for Learners* https://www.mineolagrows.com_

This website was developed by Mineola Public Schools in New York. It has a variety of student videos that you can access. (*Meet Your Neurons* is one of my favorites!) It also includes a documentary for schools and districts called *The Process* which highlights the journey to becoming a Growth Mindset district.

I also really like this one for middle school:

- *Recognizing Mistakes Improves Our Brain! | Middle School Lesson 1* (6 minutes) https://www.youtube.com/watch?v=blwujFXq-HI

Ted Talks

- *The Power of Yet: Carol S. Dweck* (11 minutes) https://www.youtube.com/watch?v=J-swZaKN2Ic

This talk for educators and parents provides an overview of growth and fixed mindset, praising process, and using the word "yet" to change students' mindset.

- *Never, Ever Give Up: Diana Nyad* (15:35 minutes)
  https://www.youtube.com/watch?v=Zx8uYIfUvh4

Swimmer Diana Nyad achieved her lifelong goal of swimming 100 miles from Cuba to Florida. She shares the obstacles and the ways that she persevered to accomplish her goal in this video.

- *Labels Limit Learning: James Nottingham* (18 minutes)
  https://www.youtube.com/watch?v=viHaslVc9cc

Educational consultant James Nottingham discusses the issue of labeling children—good and bad—and offers alternatives to focus on student progress and to use labels to describe actions rather than people.

Books for Children

- *Your Fantastic Elastic Brain* by JoAnn Deak—this illustrated picture book does an excellent job of making neuroscience fun and engaging.
- *Good Night to Your Fantastic Elastic Brain* by JoAnn Deak and Terrence Deak—this sequel provides additional

information about the brain and how it benefits from sleep in a relatable, entertaining way.

- *The Owner's Manual for Driving Your Adolescent Brain* by JoAnn Deak and Terrence Deak–this book grapples with teenage-specific brain questions while maintaining the same engaging style as their books for younger children.
- *Neurology for Kids* by Betty Nguyen and Brandon Pham—a simple picture book for ages 6–10 written by doctors, this guide includes a good explanation of neural connections and the various parts of the brain.
- *My First Book About the Brain* by Donald M. Silver and Patricia J. Wynne—this is a coloring book approach, suitable for ages 8–12.
- *How to Be a Genius* by DK Publishing—comprehensive and engaging, this book includes wonderful graphics to illustrate the work of the brain; we just wish it had a different title!
- *The Big Brain Book: How It Works and All Its Quirks* by Leanne Boucher Gill—this is a large and comprehensive encyclopedia about the brain and how it works that includes lots of engaging and helpful graphics.
- *Neurocomic* by Matteo Farinella and Hana Ros—a graphic novel written and illustrated by two neuroscientists, this book is a delight for teenagers and adults alike.
- *The Brain is Kind of a Big Deal* by Nick Seluk—a wonderfully illustrated and captivating book that gets the brain science right.
- *Nothing You Can't Do! The Secret Power of Growth Mindsets* by Mary Cay Ricci—a funny, cartoon-illustrated, interactive non-fiction book for kids ages 8–13.

Other Resources

- Website: www.marycayricci.com

Appendix A: Websites, Videos, and Books

- My Ed Expert: https://myedexpert.com/search/?_sf_s =Ricci

- Mindset-dedicated Twitter (X) and Threads @MaryCayR

APPENDIX B

PARENT NEWSLETTER BLURBS

Parent Newsletter Blurbs in English

First Newsletter Installment

One way that parents can really help their children is by carefully choosing the words that are used when they praise them. Every word parents say and action they perform sends a message to their children. These words and actions tell children how to think about themselves. Parents should always praise their child's effort instead of praising accomplishments. The following table includes some examples.

Do Not Say	Do Say
You are really athletic!	You really work hard and pay attention when you are on that field!
You are so smart!	You work hard in school, and it shows!
Your drawing is wonderful; you are my little artist.	I can see you have been practicing your drawing; what a great improvement!

You are a great athlete. You could be the next Lionel Messi!	Keep practicing, and you will see great results!
You always get good grades; that makes me happy.	When you put forth effort, it really shows in your grades. You should be so proud of yourself. We are proud of you!

So the next time you are ready to praise your child, stop and think about how to use that opportunity to praise his or her effort instead of accomplishments.

Second Newsletter Installment

In the last installment of [*name of school newsletter*], parents were given suggestions about ways to praise their children. Research suggests that parents should think twice about praising their kids for being "smart" or "talented," because this may foster a *fixed mindset*. Instead, if we encourage our kids' efforts and acknowledge their persistence and hard work, then we will support their development of a *growth mindset*. Children with a growth mindset believe that with effort and persistence they can learn and achieve in school. A growth mindset will better equip them to persevere and pick themselves up when things do not go their way. Parents should also examine their own belief systems. Do you have a growth mindset? Do you believe that with effort, persistence, and motivation your children can achieve their goals?

Dr. Carol Dweck, an educational researcher states,

> Parents should not shield their children from challenges, mistakes, and struggles. Instead, parents should teach children to love challenges. They can say things like "This is hard. What fun!" or "This is too easy. It's no fun." They should teach their children to embrace mistakes, "Oooh, here's an interesting mistake. What should we do next?" And they should teach them to love effort: "That was a fantastic struggle. You really stuck to it and made

great progress" or "This will take a lot of effort—
boy, will it be fun."

Some parents need to work at having a growth mindset. It takes
time and practice, but it is well worth it when you see the difference
that it makes in your children!

Parent Newsletter Blurbs in Spanish

First Newsletter Installment

Una forma en que los padres pueden realmente ayudar a sus
hijos es escogiendo cuidadosamente las palabras que usan para elo-
giarlos. Todas las palabras que los padres utilizan y sus acciones
transmiten un mensaje a sus hijos. Dichas palabras y acciones
manifiestan a sus hijos cómo pensar acerca de sí mismos. Los padres
siempre deben elogiar el esfuerzo de sus hijos, en vez de elogiar sola-
mente sus logros. Por ejemplo:

No Diga	Diga
¡Eres un verdadero deportista!	¡Realmente te esmeras mucho y prestas atención cuando estás en el campo de juego!
¡Eres tan inteligente!	¡Trabajas mucho en la escuela y se nota!
Tu dibujo es maravilloso; tú eres mi pequeño artista.	Se nota que has estado practicando dibujar; ¡cómo has mejorado!
Eres un gran deportista. ¡Tú podrías ser el próximo Lionel Messi! (o usando el nombre de otro deportista)	¡Continúa practicando y verás grandes resultados!
Tú siempre tienes buenas calificaciones; eso me alegra mucho.	Cuando te esfuerzas, realmente se nota en tus calificaciones. Deberías sentirte muy orgulloso/a de ti mismo/a. ¡Estamos orgullosos de ti!

Así que la próxima vez que usted vaya a elogiar a su hijo/a, deténgase y piense cómo usar esa oportunidad para elogiar su esfuerzo y no sus logros.

Second Newsletter Installment

En el último fascículo de [*nombre del boletín de noticias de la escuela*], se ofrecieron sugerencias a los padres sobre cómo elogiar a sus hijos. Las investigaciones sugieren que los padres deberían pensar dos veces antes de elogiar a sus hijos por ser "inteligentes" o "talentosos", ya que esto puede fomentar una *actitud fija*. En cambio, si estimulamos el esfuerzo en nuestros hijos, si damos reconocimiento a la perseverancia y al trabajo fuerte, apoyaremos su evolución hacia una *actitud de crecimiento*. Los niños que poseen una actitud de crecimiento pasan a creer que con esfuerzo y perseverancia aprenderán y podrán desempeñarse bien en sus estudios. Una actitud de crecimiento los equipará mejor para tener perseverancia y para levantar el ánimo cuando las cosas no son como ellos desearían. Los padres deberían también examinar sus propias formas de pensar. ¿Posee usted una actitud de crecimiento? ¿Cree usted que con esfuerzo, perseverancia y motivación sus hijos pueden alcanzar sus metas? La Dra. Carol Dweck, investigadora educacional, manifiesta,

> Los padres no deben proteger a sus hijos de los desafíos, errores y luchas. En su lugar, los padres deberían enseñar a sus hijos a amar el desafío. Ellos pueden decir cosas como "Esto es difícil. ¡Qué divertido!" o "Esto es demasiado fácil. No es divertido." Ellos deben enseñar a sus hijos a aceptar los errores, "Ah, aquí hay un error interesante. ¿Qué deberíamos hacer ahora?" Y ellos deberían enseñarles a amar el esfuerzo: "Esa fue una lucha fantástica. Realmente te mantuviste en pie y lograste un gran progreso." O, "Esto va a tomar mucho esfuerzo—pero mira que será divertido."

Algunos padres necesitan trabajar para lograr tener una Actitud de Crecimiento. ¡Eso toma tiempo y práctica, pero realmente vale la pena cuando se nota la diferencia que ha ce en sus hijos!

Printed in the United States
by Baker & Taylor Publisher Services